Salmon Shrimps Cookbook

This volume contains 2 books in 1. Learn many new, low budget, quick and easy ideas. Increase your muscles and balance your weight, with this high protein supply recipes. Boost your energy and increase your family body and mind healing

Ernest Pescara

Table of Contents
Book 1 and 2:

4

Welcome, dear!

This is my offer to your cooking style.

This cookbook is the realization of my research on how to eat tasty and healthy food at the meantime.
My purpose is to increase your energies and to let you live a lighter life, without the junk of the globalised kitchen.

In here, you'll find my knowledge on how to create delicious dishes with salmon.

Jump into a worldwide discovery of good food and natural-feed animals, with many recipes for a varied diet.

Nevertheless, you'll learn new techniques, discover tastes of all around the world and improve your skills.
Let yourself be inspired by the worldwide traditions, twisted by a proper chef.

Each of these dishes is thought to:

1 – Let you understand how to work with the Salmon

This majestic animal is offered in various presentations of different cultures, to show you how the same ingredient can change from dish to dish.

2 – Balance your weight with different cooking methods

As soon as you learn different ways to cook your fish, you'll discover an entire world of new ideas.
Salmon will never bore you again!

3 – Amaze your friends starting from the smell

Once your friends will come to dinner, they will be in love with your food even before to see your creation.

The King Salmon Cookbook

Gain creativity, tastefulness and a perfect weight balance with these delicious, quick and easy recipes, thought to improve your muscles and boost your mental energy. Expand your beginner skills and learn step by step how to use this amazing fish

Ernest Pescara

King Salmon Recipes

Honey-Glazed Salmon Steaks

Serves 2 pax

Ingredients

- 1 tbsp runny honey
- 1 garlic clove, peeled and crushed
- Salt and freshly ground black pepper
- 1 cup Olive oil
- 1 tbsp balsamic vinegar
- 1 tbsp Dijon mustard
- 2 salmon steaks

Procedure

1. Mix together the vinegar, mustard, honey, garlic and seasoning in a bowl.
2. Brush over both sides of the salmon and leave in the fridge for about an hour.
3. Heat a ridged frying pan to a very high heat, then rub it with a little oil.
4. Sear the steaks for about 3 minutes on each side, turning only once. The fish is cooked if it flakes easily when lightly prised with a fork.
5. The cooking time may vary depending on the thickness of the salmon steaks and how you like them cooked.
6. Remove from the grill, brush with any remaining glaze.
7. Serve.

Salmon and Spinaches Salad

Serves 2 pax

Ingredients

- 1 cup Dried cranberries
- 1 cup Canola oil
- 1 tbsp Balsamic vinaigrette
- 2 Avocado
- 1 Salmon fillet
- 1 oz Spinach
- 1 cup Sunflower kernels
- 1 cup Walnuts
- Salt and Pepper

Procedure

1. Place a large skillet and oil on a moderate fire and place in the salmon fillets. Sprinkle with pepper and salt.
2. Cook it until the fish flakes easily.
3. Place your spinach in a bowl and pour in the vinaigrette.
4. Toss to evenly coat and serve on plates.
5. Place the salmon on the spinach and top with the remaining ingredients.

Salmon in 5 Spices

Serves 2 pax

Ingredients

- 2 (6-ounce) salmon fillets, washed and patted dry
- 2 teaspoons lime juice
- 1/2teaspoon Chinese 5-spice powder
- 1 tablespoon unsalted butter
- 1 cup Vegetable oil

Procedure

1. Using paper towels, wipe a thin coat of vegetable oil over a broiler pan.
2. Preheat your broiler on high, with the rack set on the upper third of the oven.
3. Melt the butter using low heat in a small deep cooking pan. Mix in the 5-spice powder and lime juice; keep warm.
4. Put the salmon on the broiler pan, skin side up. Broil for two to 4 minutes or until the skin is crunchy.
5. Turn the salmon over and broil two minutes more or until done to your preference.
6. Move the salmon to 2 plates and spoon the butter sauce over the top.

Roasted Salmon Filets

Serves 4 pax

Ingredients

- 1 Tbsp Lime juice
- 1 Tbsp Freshly grated ginger
- 1 Tbsp Serrano chile pepper
- 1 Tbsp Olive oil
- 4x 4 oz Salmon filets
- 1 Tbsp Brown sugar blend
- 2 Tbsp Soy sauce

Procedure

1. Set the oven temperature at 375° Fahrenheit.
2. Stir together all ingredients except the salmon, then pour it over the salmon in a dish small enough so the marinade will cover each side of the fish.
3. Refrigerate to marinate for 30 minutes. Preheat the grill.
4. Grill the salmon for four to six minutes per side. Discard the remaining marinade.
5. If you prefer to bake this, prepare a baking dish with cooking oil spray.
6. Place it in the dish and bake for eight to ten minutes per side until just opaque.

Whole-Wheat Salmon Spaghetti

Serves 6 pax

Ingredients

- 1 (15-ounce) can cannellini beans, rinsed
- 1 onion, chopped fine
- 1 pound whole-wheat spaghetti
- 2 pounds curly-leaf spinach, stemmed and cut into 1-inch pieces
- 5 ounces Parmesan cheese, grated (1 cup), plus extra for serving
- 3 tablespoons extra-virgin olive oil, plus extra for serving
- 1 Salmon fillet
- 1/2teaspoon red pepper flakes
- 3/4 cup pitted kalamata olives, chopped coarse
- 3/4 cup vegetable broth
- 1 (14.5-ounce) can diced tomatoes, drained
- 8 garlic cloves, peeled (5 sliced thin along the length, 3 minced)
- Salt and pepper

Procedure

1. Cook oil and sliced garlic in 12-inch straight-sided sauté pan on moderate heat, stirring frequently, until garlic turns golden but not brown, approximately three minutes. Use a slotted spoon to move garlic to plate coated using paper towels and season lightly with salt; set aside.

2. Put in onion to oil left in pan and cook on moderate heat till they become tender and lightly browned, 5 to 7 minutes. Mix in minced garlic, pepper flakes, salmon and cook until aromatic, approximately half a minute.

3. Put in half of spinach and cook, tossing occasionally, until starting to wilt, approximately two minutes. Put in remaining spinach, broth, tomatoes, and 3/4 teaspoon salt and bring to simmer.

4. Decrease heat to medium, cover (pan will be very full), and cook, tossing occasionally, until spinach is completely wilted, about 10 minutes (mixture will be somewhat soupy). Remove from the heat, mix in beans and olives.

5. In the meantime, bring 4 quarts water to boil in large pot. Put in pasta and 1 tablespoon salt and cook, stirring frequently, until just shy of al dente. Reserve 1/2cup cooking water, then drain pasta and return it to pot.
6. Put in greens mixture and cook on moderate heat, tossing to combine, until pasta absorbs most of liquid, approximately two minutes.
7. Remove from the heat, mix in Parmesan. Sprinkle with salt and pepper to taste and regulate consistency with reserved cooking water as required.
8. Serve, sprinkling individual portions with garlic chips and extra Parmesan and drizzling with extra oil.

Zucchini Farfalle and Salmon

Ingredients

- 2 garlic cloves, minced
- 1 Salmon fillet
- 1/4 cup chopped fresh mint
- 1/2cup pitted kalamata olives, quartered
- 18 pounds farfalle
- 1 red onion, chopped fine
- 1 teaspoon grated lemon zest plus 1 tablespoon juice
- 12 ounces grape tomatoes, halved
- 3 pounds zucchini and/or summer squash, halved along the length and sliced 1/2inch thick
- 3 teaspoons red wine vinegar
- 12 ounces feta cheese, crumbled
- 4 tablespoons extra-virgin olive oil
- Kosher salt and pepper

Procedure

1. Toss squash with 1 tablespoon salt and allow to drain using a colander for 30 minutes. Pat squash dry using paper towels and carefully wipe away any residual salt.

2. Heat 1 tablespoon oil in 12-inch non-stick frying pan on high heat until just smoking. Put in half of squash and salmon and cook, stirring intermittently, until golden brown and mildly charred, 5 to 7 minutes, reducing heat if frying pan begins to scorch; move to large plate.

3. Repeat with 1 tablespoon oil and remaining squash; move to plate.

4. Heat 1 tablespoon oil in now-empty frying pan on moderate heat until it starts to shimmer. Put in onion and cook till they become tender and lightly browned, 5 to 7 minutes.

5. Mix in garlic, lemon zest, and 1/2teaspoon pepper and cook until aromatic, approximately half a minute. Mix in squash and cook until heated through, approximately half a minute.

6. In the meantime, bring 4 quarts water to boil in large pot. Put in pasta and 1 tablespoon salt and cook, stirring frequently, until al dente.

7. Reserve 1/2cup cooking water, then drain pasta and return it to pot. Put in squash mixture, tomatoes, olives, mint, vinegar, lemon juice, and remaining 2 tablespoons oil and toss to combine.

8. Sprinkle with salt and pepper to taste and serve.

Grilled Salmon, Chilean Sauce

Serves 4 pax

Ingredients

- 1 (13 by 9 inch) disposable aluminum roasting pan
- 1 teaspoon grated lime zest
- 6 tablespoons juice (3 limes)
- 2 garlic cloves, minced
- 3 tablespoons chopped fresh cilantro
- 4 tablespoons vegetable oil
- 2 tablespoons unsalted butter
- 1/2teaspoon ground cumin
- 1 (10 ounce) skin on salmon steaks, 2 inches thick
- Salt and pepper

Procedure

1. Pat salmon steaks dry using paper towels. Working with 1 steak at a time, cautiously trim 11/2inches of skin from 1 tail.

2. Firmly wrap other tail around skinned portion and tie steaks using a kitchen twine. Season salmon with salt and pepper and brush both sides with oil. Mix lime zest and juice, butter, garlic, cumin, and 1/8 teaspoon salt in disposable pan.

3. On a GAS GRILL: Set all burners to high, cover, and heat grill until hot, approximately fifteen minutes. Leave primary burner on high and turn off other burner(s).

4. Clean cooking grate, then constantly brush grate with well oiled paper towels until black and shiny, five to ten times.

5. Put salmon on hotter part of grill. Cook until browned on both sides, two to three minutes per side.

6. In the meantime, set disposable pan on cooler part of grill and cook until butter has melted, approximately 2 minutes.

7. Move salmon to pan and gently turn to coat. Cook salmon (covered if using gas) until center is still translucent when checked with tip of paring knife and records 125 degrees (for medium rare), six to fourteen minutes, turning salmon and rotating pan midway through grilling.
8. Move salmon to platter; remove twine. Whisk cilantro into sauce left in pan.
9. Sprinkle sauce over salmon before you serve.

Guaca Salsa for Salmon

Serves 6 pax

Ingredients

- 1/4 teaspoon salt
- 1/8 teaspoon fresh ground black pepper
- 1/2avocado, pitted and diced
- 1/4 cup fresh cilantro, chopped
- 1 large tomato, diced
- 1/4 cup red onion, diced
- 1/2jalapeno pepper, minced
- 5 tablespoons fresh squeezed lime juice
- 1 pinch cayenne pepper

Procedure

1. Combine tomato, onion, minced jalapeno, lime juice, salt and pepper in bowl.
2. Add avocado, cilantro and cayenne.
3. Stir until well mixed.
4. Refrigerate.

Salmon Steaks, Chard and Coconut Sauce

Serves 4 pax

Ingredients

- 1 (2 inches) fresh ginger piece
- 4 salmon steaks or fillets
- Sea salt and freshly ground black pepper
- A handful of Chard, when held by the stalks
- A glug of olive oil
- 1 large onion, peeled and thinly sliced
- 4 tomatoes, deseeded and chopped
- 1 tsp sugar
- 1/2 mug coconut milk
- 1/2 mug water
- Juice of 1 lime
- 1 handful of chopped fresh coriander

Procedure

1. Slice the ginger and cut into slivers (it's not necessary to peel the ginger – just cut off any tough bits). Season the salmon with salt and pepper and set aside.

2. Strip the chard leaves from the stalks and roughly chop the leaves. Dice the stalks into small pieces.

3. Heat the oil in a wide, deep frying pan over a medium heat. Add the onion, ginger and chard stems and cook, stirring occasionally, for about 5 minutes.

4. Add the chopped tomatoes and the sugar and continue to cook for another 4–5 minutes. Add the coconut milk and water and season well with salt and pepper. Stir, bring to the boil, then simmer over a low heat for a further 15 minutes.

5. Stir in the chard leaves, squeeze the lime over them and arrange the salmon pieces in a single layer over the top of the sauce. Spoon some of the liquid over the fish.

6. Cover with a tight-fitting lid, return to a medium heat, and simmer for about 10 minutes, or until the fish is just cooked through.
7. To serve, lift the fish and chard sauce onto a hot serving dish.
8. Spoon the remaining liquid over the top of the fish, garnish with coriander and serve immediately with rice.

Grilled Medallions of Salmon

Serves 6 pax

Ingredients

- 1 large salmon fillet
- 3 tbsp extra-virgin olive oil

Procedure

1. Preheat grill.
2. Brush salmon liberally with oil. Grill salmon, brushing with oil as needed. When salmon is done, cut into medallions.
3. Garnish linguini pasta with salmon medallions.
4. Serve immediately.

Salmon Tartare and Avocado

Ingredients

- 4 ounces smoked Alaskan salmon sliced thin
- 1 garlic clove, chopped very fine
- 1/4 teaspoon fresh ground black pepper
- 1 pinch cayenne pepper
- 3 shallots, chopped very fine
- 1 tablespoon fresh squeezed lemon juice
- 1/2teaspoon salt
- 14 ounces fresh Alaskan salmon fillet
- 4 drops Worcestershire sauce

Procedure

1. Remove skin from salmon. Cut fillet and smoked salmon slices into 1/4" strips.
2. Combine salmon in bowl with all other ingredients. Mix until thoroughly combined.
3. Line four 3" ramekins with plastic wrap, let edges project.
4. Divide tartare mix evenly amongst ramekins. Press tops lightly until smooth.
5. Turn ramekins out onto serving plates. Remove plastic wrap.
6. Serve.

Grilled Salmon, Pesto and Watercress

Serves 4 pax

Ingredients

- 1/4 cup chopped peeled fresh ginger
- 1/4 teaspoon cayenne pepper
- 7 tablespoons vegetable oil
- Salt and freshly ground black pepper to taste
- 1 cup chopped fresh cilantro
- ½ cup chopped green onions
- 1/3 cup salted roasted macadamia nuts
- 4 x 6-ounce pieces salmon fillet
- 1 large garlic clove, minced
- 3 tablespoons olive oil
- 2 bunches of watercress, coarse stems discarded and the watercress rinsed but not spun dry

Procedure

1. Combine first 5 ingredients in food processor. Blend until nuts are finely chopped. Add 6 tablespoons oil and process until well blended. Season to taste with salt and pepper.

2. Prepare grill.

3. Brush salmon with remaining 1 tablespoon vegetable oil and sprinkle with salt and pepper to taste. Grill salmon on an oiled rack set 5 to 6 inches over glowing coals until just cooked through, about 5 minutes on each side.

4. Meanwhile, in a large heavy skillet sauté the garlic in the olive oil over moderately high heat for 30 seconds, or until it is fragrant.

5. Add the watercress and stir the mixture until it is combined well. Sauté the watercress, covered, for 2 to 3 minutes, or until it is just wilted, and Season to taste with salt and pepper.

6. To serve, put sautéed watercress in the center of 4 plates. Top with the salmon and spoon pesto around. Serve basmati rice alongside.

7. Serve with basmati rice.

Phyllo Salmon, Shiitake and Champagne

Serves 6 pax

Ingredients

- 1/2teaspoon freshly ground black pepper
- 3 garlic cloves, minced
- 1 lemon, thinly sliced
- 3 pounds salmon fillet
- 1/4 cup chopped scallions
- 15 x 6 x 3/8-inch cedar grilling plank
- ½ cup rice vinegar
- ½ cup low-sodium soy sauce
- 4 tablespoons honey
- 1 teaspoon ground ginger
- 1 tablespoon sesame seeds, toasted

Procedure

1. Immerse and soak the plank in water 1 hour; drain.
2. To prepare grill for indirect grilling, heat one side of the grill to high heat.
3. Combine vinegar and the next 6 ingredients (vinegar through lemon) in a large zip-top plastic bag; seal.
4. Shake to combine. Add fish; seal. Marinate in refrigerator 30 minutes, turning once.
5. Place plank on grill rack over high heat; grill 5 minutes or until lightly charred. Carefully turn plank over; move to cool side of grill.
6. Remove fish from marinade; discard marinade. Place fish, skin side down, on charred side of plank.
7. Cover and grill 15 minutes or until fish flakes easily when tested with a fork.
8. To serve, place on bed of Pickled Ginger and Watercress Salad (recipe follows) on 6 plates.
9. Top with portions of salmon and sprinkle with scallions and sesame seeds.

Pickled Ginger and Watercress Salad

Serves 6 pax

Ingredients

- 1 tablespoon fresh lime juice or rice wine vinegar
- 1 tablespoon canola oil
- 1 teaspoon honey
- 1 clove garlic, crushed
- 1/8 teaspoon kosher salt
- 1 tablespoon liquid from a jar of picked ginger
- Freshly ground black pepper to taste
- 6 cups stemmed, washed and dried watercress
- 4 scallions, chopped
- 1/3 cup drained pickled ginger

Procedure

1. With the side of a chef's knife, mash garlic with salt.
2. Place in a small bowl or a jar with a tightfitting lid.
3. Add ginger liquid, lime juice (or vinegar), oil, honey and pepper; whisk or shake until blended.
4. Place watercress, scallions and pickled ginger in a large bowl.
5. Just before serving, toss with dressing.

Seafood Linguini and Salmon

Ingredients

- 8 ounces clams (cooked, drained and chopped)
- 1 pound fresh scallops (raw)
- 1 cup lobster stock
- 18 pounds fresh linguine
- 1 ounce butter
- 8 ounces mussel meat
- 1 cup heavy cream

Procedure

1. Cook linguine in pot of salted water with butter. Drain and set aside when al dente
2. Heat lobster stock until reduced in half.
3. Add heavy cream and reduce until slightly thickened. Whip lightly.
4. Add cooked linguini and drained seafood. Stir gently 10 minutes.
5. Serve immediately when seafood is done and sauce is creamy.

Salmon and Sweet Potatoes

Ingredients

- 2 Limes, 1 zested and juiced, one cut into wedges
- 3 Tbsp Mayonnaise
- 4 tsp Olive oil
- 1.25 lbs Salmon fillet, quartered
- 4 cups Broccoli florets
- 1 tsp Chili powder
- ½ cup Cilantro, chopped
- 1/4 cup Feta
- Salt to taste
- 2 Sweet potatoes, peeled and cubed

Procedure

1. Begin preheating your oven up to a temperature of 425° F. Then, prepare a sheet pan with grease. Mix mayonnaise and chili powder and set aside.
2. Season sweet potatoes and spread onto sheet pan to roast, drizzling olive oil onto them. Roast for 15 minutes.
3. Season broccoli and place onto sheet pan alongside salmon. Spread mayonnaise mixture on the salmon and bake until it easily flakes.
4. Add lime zest and juice to remaining mayonnaise and mix.
5. Serve salmon with cheese and cilantro on top, with a side of potatoes and broccoli.
6. Drizzle mayonnaise sauce on top and serve with lime wedges.

Roses of Norwegian Salmon

Serves 8 pax

Ingredients

- 16 ounces smoked Norwegian salmon slices

Procedure

1. Lay smoked salmon flat.
2. With a fillet knife, cut a 3-inch-long strip 1 inch wide.
3. Cut the strip from the edge of the fish, so the naturally uneven edge is part of the strip.
4. Roll the first inch of the strip tightly to form the center of a rose.
5. Roll the rest of the strip more loosely around the center.
6. Pinch together at the cut edge, leaving the thin, uneven edge to form the petals.
7. Hold the rose at the base.
8. With the tip of the fillet knife, gently peel back the rolled salmon just enough to open up the rose.
9. Repeat as necessary until all the salmon is used.

Pan Seared Salmon

Serves 6 pax

Ingredients

- 1/4 cup extra virgin olive oil
- Salt and freshly ground black pepper
- 6 x 6 oz center-cut salmon fillets
- 1/4 cup fresh lemon juice

Procedure

1. Darne is the middle cut of a large fish.
2. Place salmon darnes in a shallow bowl. Add lemon juice and olive oil. Season to taste with salt and pepper.
3. Toss until salmon is thoroughly coated. Let stand 15 minutes.
4. Place salmon skin side down in a skillet. Sear salmon 3 minutes on medium-high heat.
5. Shake pan and carefully loosen salmon with a spatula.
6. Lower heat to medium. Cover skillet and cook 4 minutes. Salmon darnes are done when skin is crisp and flesh medium rare.
7. Serve on bed of chunky fruit (recipe follows).

Chunky Fruit

Ingredients

- 3 tablespoons cilantro, chopped
- 1 large jalapeno pepper, seeded and minced
- 2 tablespoons fresh ginger, minced
- 6 tablespoons fresh squeezed orange juice
- 2 small limes fresh squeezed juice
- 2 teaspoons dried mint
- 1 large papaya, seeded and cubed
- 2 bananas, sliced
- 1 kiwi fruit, peeled and chopped
- 2 pints strawberries, quartered

Procedure

1. Mix orange juice, lime juice, zest, mint, cilantro, jalapeno and ginger together in a large bowl.
2. Add fruit. Toss well and refrigerate overnight.
3. To serve, divide fruit salad between 6 plates.
4. Top each fruit bed with the Salmon.

Lychee and Fennel Chutney

Serves 6 pax

Ingredients

- 2 teaspoons turmeric powder
- 2 tablespoons mustard seeds
- 10 lychees
- 4 tablespoons fennel seeds
- 3 tablespoons fenugreek seeds
- 2 tablespoons red chili powder
- 2 cups mustard
- 1 cup evo oil
- Salt to taste

Procedure

1. Clean lychees and chop into 3/4" cubes. Rub with turmeric powder and salt. Let stand 30 minutes.
2. Drain excess moisture.
3. Grind fenugreek, fennel and mustard seeds to a coarse powder.
4. Heat mustard oil to smoking point. Remove from heat and let stand.
5. Mix ground seeds with red chili powder. Add half of the mustard oil to the powder mixture. Rub spice and oil mixture to lychee cubes until thoroughly mixed.
6. Place lychees in earthenware jar. Pour in other half of mustard oil. Add salt to taste and stir well. Cover jar with muslin cloth. Let stand 6 days in sunlight, stirring twice daily.
7. Continue to stir contents of jar twice daily for two weeks.
8. Serve as relish.

Steamed Potatoes

Ingredients

- 2 tablespoons fresh parsley, chopped
- 3 tablespoons extra-virgin olive oil
- 2 pounds new potatoes
- 2 tablespoons green onions, diced fine
- 1 garlic clove, minced
- Salt and freshly ground black pepper

Procedure

1. Pour an inch of water in steamer. Heat on medium-high heat.
2. Wash potatoes and place in the steamer basket. Sprinkle with a little sea salt.
3. When water simmers, place steamer basket on pot and cover. Cook 20 minutes. Potatoes are done when tender.
4. While steaming potatoes, heat olive oil and minced garlic in small skillet on low heat. Set aside when fragrant.
5. Remove potatoes from steaming basket. Place in large bowl. Add oil and garlic mixture, green onions and parsley.
6. Season to taste with salt and pepper. Toss potatoes until well coated.
7. Serve hot.

Roasted Salmon in Salsa Verde

Serves 4 pax

Ingredients

- 1 tablespoon lime juice, plus lime wedges for serving
- 1 teaspoon ground coriander
- 1/4 cup minced fresh cilantro
- 1 (2 pound) skin on salmon fillet, 2 inches thick
- 1 jalapeño chile, stemmed, halved, and seeded
- 1 poblano chile, stemmed, seeded, and chopped
- 2 scallions, chopped
- 12 ounces tomatillos, husks and stems removed, washed well, dried, and quartered
- 3 tablespoons plus 2 teaspoons extra virgin olive oil
- 2 teaspoons chopped fresh oregano
- 2 garlic cloves, peeled
- Salt and pepper

Procedure

1. Adjust oven racks to lowest position and 6 inches from broiler element and heat broiler. Coat baking sheet with aluminium foil.
2. Toss tomatillos, poblano, jalapeño, 1 tablespoon oil, garlic, oregano, coriander, 1/4 teaspoon salt, and 1/4 teaspoon pepper together, then spread onto readied sheet.
3. Broil vegetables on upper rack until tomatillos and jalapeños are browned, ten to twelve minutes, stirring once in a while.
4. Move broiled vegetables to blender and allow to cool slightly. Put in 2 tablespoons cilantro, scallions, lime juice, and 1 tablespoon oil and blend until the desired smoothness is achieved, approximately one minute.
5. In the meantime, place clean rimmed baking sheet on lower oven rack and heat oven to 500 degrees.
6. Cut salmon crosswise into 4 fillets. Using sharp knife, make 4 or 5 shallow slashes, approximately an inch apart, through skin of each fillet, being cautious not to cut into flesh.

7. Pat salmon dry using paper towels, rub with remaining 2 teaspoons oil, and sprinkle with salt and pepper.

8. Reduce oven temperature to 275 degrees and remove preheated baking sheet. Cautiously place salmon, skin side down, on baking sheet.

9. Roast on lower rack until center is still translucent when checked with tip of paring knife and records 125 degrees (for medium rare), 9 to 13 minutes.

10. Move salmon to plates, spoon some of sauce over top and drizzle with remaining 2 tablespoons minced cilantro.

11. Serve with rest of the sauce and lime wedges.

Salmon Terrine and Salmon Caviar Sauce

Ingredients

- 1 tablespoon lemon zest
- 2 tablespoons lemon juice
- 1/3 cup fresh dill, finely chopped
- 1 pound sliced smoked Norwegian salmon
- 2 cups cream cheese
- 1/4 cup cream
- 2 tablespoons capers
- Freshly ground black pepper

Procedure

1. Place cream cheese, cream, lemon zest, lemon juice, dill and capers in a food processor. Season to taste with pepper and combine. Butter a 6 cups terrine pan.

2. Line base and sides with plastic wrap overhanging two inches at ends. Layer enough smoked salmon to cover bottom of pan. Layer 1/3 cup cream cheese mixture equally over salmon.

3. Repeat layering process until all the salmon is used. The top layer should be salmon.

4. Fold plastic wrap over salmon, pressing down gently. Refrigerate overnight.

5. Before serving, turn onto a platter and remove wrap. Trim ends and cut into slices.

6. Drizzle with red salmon caviar sauce (recipe follows).

7. Serve.

Red Salmon Caviar Sauce

Serves 6 pax

Ingredients

- ½ cup mayonnaise
- 4 tablespoons fresh dill, chopped
- 1 pinch white pepper
- 1 cup sour cream
- 8 ounces crème fraiche
- 3 ounces red salmon caviar

Procedure

1. Combine sour cream, creme fraiche, mayonnaise, dill, and white pepper in a bowl. Stir well.
2. Carefully mix in caviar.
3. Cover and refrigerate 1 hour.
4. Drizzle over salmon terrine (recipe above).

Seafood Stuffed Salmon

Serves 12 pax

Ingredients

- 2 cups cooked long grain rice
- 1 package (8 ounces) imitation crabmeat
- 3 tablespoons cream cheese, softened
- 5 tablespoons butter, melted
- 12 salmon fillets (8 ounces each and 1-1/2 inches thick)
- 4 tablespoons olive oil
- 2 teaspoons dill weed
- 2 teaspoons salt
- 2 garlic cloves, minced
- 1/2teaspoon each dried basil, marjoram, oregano, thyme and rosemary, crushed
- 1/2teaspoon celery seed, crushed

Procedure

1. Preheat an oven to 400°F.
2. Mix celery seed, rosemary, thyme, oregano, marjoram, basil, garlic, butter, cream cheese, crab and rice in a big bowl.
3. Horizontally cut a pocket, within 1/2-in. from opposite side, in each fillet. Use stuffing mixture to fill; use toothpicks to secure.
4. Put salmon on 2 (15 x 10 x 1 -in) greased baking pans; brush oil. Sprinkle salt and dill.
5. Bake till fish just starts to easily flake with a fork for 18-22 minutes.
6. Before serving, discard toothpicks.

Salmon and Strawberry Basil Relish

Serves 6 pax

Ingredients

- 1/4 teaspoon salt
- 6 x 4 ounces salmon fillets
- 1 tablespoon butter, melted
- 1/8 teaspoon freshly ground pepper

For the Relish:

- 1 tablespoon honey
- 1 cup finely chopped fresh strawberries
- 1 tablespoon minced fresh basil
- Dash freshly ground pepper

Procedure

1. Brush melted butter on fillets; sprinkle with pepper and salt.
2. On medium-high heat, heat a big skillet. Add fillets in batches if needed, skin side up; cook till fish just starts to easily flake with a fork or for 2-3 minutes per side.
3. Toss pepper, honey, basil and strawberries in a small bowl.
4. Serve salmon with relish.

Layered Salmon and Cobb Salad

Serves 6 pax

Ingredients

- 2 teaspoons chopped fresh dill
- Salt and ground black pepper to taste
- 3 cups fresh green beans, trimmed
- 3/4 cup buttermilk
- 1/4 cup mayonnaise
- 5 hard-boiled eggs, halved
- 6 slices cooked bacon, cut into thin strips
- 3 spring onions, thinly sliced
- 2 tablespoons white wine vinegar
- ½ clove garlic, crushed
- 6x 5 pounds salmon fillets
- ½ teaspoon vegetable oil
- 4 cups chopped green leaf lettuce
- 1 pound tomatoes, cut into bite-sized pieces
- 1 (15 ounce) can corn, drained
- 2 cucumbers, halved and sliced

Procedure

1. In a jar, mix garlic, buttermilk, white wine vinegar, and mayonnaise. Seal the jar and then shake thoroughly. Mix in pepper, dill, and salt. Chill the dressing.

2. Put a steamer insert in a saucepan and add water until just below bottom of the steamer. Heat the water to boil. Place in green beans, cover the pan and then steam for about 4 to 5 minutes until tender. Drain off water and cool.

3. Preheat the grill over medium heat and coat the grate lightly with oil. Baste the salmon with the vegetable oil. Add pepper and salt to taste.

4. Cook the salmon on the grill for about 6 to 8 minutes on each side until the flesh easily flakes with a fork.

5. In a large glass trifle bowl, spread lettuce, green beans, tomatoes, corn, hard-boiled eggs and cucumbers.

6. Top with the salmon. Stud with spring onions and bacon.

7. Serve along with the dressing.

Apricot Glazed Salmon and Herb Rice

Serves 6 pax

Ingredients

- 1/3 cup apricot spreadable fruit
- ½ teaspoon grated fresh gingerroot
- 2 cups reduced-sodium chicken broth
- 1 teaspoon minced fresh thyme
- 3 tablespoons sliced almonds, toasted
- 1 cup uncooked long grain rice
- 6 x 4 ounces salmon fillets
- 1/4 teaspoon salt
- 1/8 teaspoon pepper
- 1/3 cup white wine
- 2 teaspoons butter
- 2 tablespoons chopped dried apricots
- 2 tablespoons minced fresh parsley
- 1 tablespoon minced chives

Procedure

1. Coat a 13 x 9-inch pan with cooking spray and lay salmon inside.
2. Season with pepper and salt to taste. Meanwhile, mix together spreadable fruit, ginger and wine in a small bowl. Pour mixture over the salmon.
3. Bake for 15 to 20 minutes at 375° until fish separates easily with fork.
4. While the fish is baking, combine rice, butter and broth in a small pot and bring to a boil. Turn the heat down and let it simmer, covered, 10 minutes.
5. Add the apricots and continue cooking until rice is tender and all the liquid gets absorbed, 5 to 8 minutes.
6. Mix in chives, thyme and parsley.
7. Serve rice with salmon and garnish with almonds.

Salmon and Asparagus Pasta

Ingredients

- 2 cups uncooked bow tie pasta
- 2 pounds fresh asparagus, trimmed and cut into 2-inch pieces
- 2 medium leeks (white portion only), thinly sliced
- 2 teaspoons olive oil
- 2 teaspoons cornstarch
- ½ cup water
- 4 x 1 pound salmon fillet
- ½ teaspoon salt, divided
- ½ teaspoon pepper, divided
- ½ cup chicken broth
- 2 tablespoons snipped fresh dill
- 1 tablespoon lemon juice

Procedure

1. Season the salmon with a quarter teaspoon (1/4 teaspoon) of salt and pepper. Lightly coat the grill rack using an oiled paper towel and tongs with a long handle.

2. Start grilling the salmon while covered on a medium heat or broil for about 4-6 inches from the heat for 12- 18 minutes with a fork.

3. Prepare the pasta as specified on its package. Sauté the leeks and asparagus in a large, oiled skillet until the asparagus get its tender-crisp texture. Season with the remaining salt and pepper.

4. Combine the lemon juice, broth, water, cornstarch, and dill, in a small bowl. Stir well until the mixture smoothens.

5. Add the sautéed asparagus and leeks. Boil and simmer; continuously stir until it bubbles and thickens.

6. Turn the heat to a minimum and cook for another 2 minutes longer while stirring. Drain the pasta and toss with asparagus mixture.

7. Serve with salmon.

Lemony Salmon and Basil

Serves 4 pax

Ingredients

- 1/2teaspoon salt
- 1/4 teaspoon pepper
- 3 tablespoons thinly sliced fresh basil
- 2 medium lemons, thinly sliced
- 4 x 6 ounces salmon fillets
- 2 teaspoons olive oil
- 1 tablespoon grated lemon peel
- Additional fresh basil

Procedure

1. Preheat an oven to 375°. Put salmon into an oiled 15 x 10 x 1 -in. Baking pan.
2. Drizzle with oil; sprinkle 2 tbsp. of basil, pepper, salt and lemon peel. Put lemon slices over the top.
3. Bake till fish starts to flake easily with a fork for 15-20 minutes; put extra basil over the top if desired.

Salmon and Balsamic Orange Sauce

Ingredients

- 4 teaspoons honey
- 8 x 6 ounces salmon fillets, skin removed
- 4 teaspoons grated orange zest
- 4 teaspoons balsamic vinegar
- 1 teaspoon salt

For the Sauce:

- 2 teaspoons honey
- 1 teaspoon balsamic vinegar
- 1 teaspoon cornstarch
- 1 cup orange juice
- 1/4 teaspoon salt

Procedure

1. Preheat an oven to 425°. Put ham into a 15x10x1-in. greased baking pan.
2. Mix salt, honey, vinegar and orange zest in a small bowl; spread over fillets.
3. Roast till fish just starts to easily flake with a fork for 15-18 minutes.
4. Meanwhile, combine orange juice and cornstarch in a small saucepan; boil; cook while stirring till thickened for one minute.
5. Mix in salt, vinegar and honey; serve with salmon.

Poached Salmon

Ingredients

- 1 lemon slice
- 1 sprig dill
- ½ teaspoon salt
- 1 cup water
- ½ cup dry white wine
- 1 yellow onion slice
- 4 x 6 ounces salmon fillets

Procedure

1. Mix together the wine and water in the slow cooker. Set on high to heat for 20 to 30 minutes.
2. Add the salmon, salt, dill, lemon and onion.
3. Set the cooker on high. Cover and let it cook for about 20 minutes, until the salmon becomes opaque and cooked completely according to taste.
4. Serve it hot and can also be served cold.

Elegant Smoked Salmon Strata

Ingredients

- 2 cups shredded Gruyere or Swiss cheese
- 2 cups shredded white cheddar cheese
- 10 green onions, sliced
- 4 cups cubed ciabatta bread
- 2 tablespoons butter, melted
- 2 tablespoons olive oil
- ½ pound smoked salmon or lox, coarsely chopped
- 8 large eggs
- 1/4 teaspoon pepper
- Creme fraiche or sour cream and minced chives
- 4 cups 2% milk
- 4 teaspoons Dijon mustard
- 1/4 teaspoon salt

Procedure

1. Toss bread cubes with oil and butter in a big bowl; move to a greased 13 x 9-inch baking dish.
2. Add salmon, onions and cheeses on top. In a separate bowl, whisk together pepper, salt, mustard, milk and eggs; add over top.
3. Keep in refrigerator, covered, overnight.
4. Remove from the fridge 30 minutes prior to baking. Cover the dish and bake for 30 minutes at 350°.
5. Remove cover and bake for another 25 to 30 minutes until an inserted knife in the middle exits clean.
6. Allow to stand for 10 minutes prior to serving.
7. Serve with chives and creme fraiche.

Salmon Omelets and Creme Fraiche

Serves 6 pax

Ingredients

- 2 tablespoons butter
- 6 x 1 pound salmon fillets, cooked and flaked
- 2 cups shredded Swiss cheese
- 12 large eggs
- 2 tablespoons whole milk
- Salt and pepper to taste
- 2 tablespoons snipped fresh dill
- 3/4 cup creme fraiche or sour cream
- 6 fresh dill sprigs

Procedure

1. Beat pepper, salt, milk, and eggs in a large bowl until combined.
2. For each omelet: Let a teaspoon of butter melt on medium heat in an 8-inch ovenproof skillet.
3. Add ½ cup of the egg mixture into the pan. Dust with a teaspoon of snipped dill, 1/2cup of cheese, and 1/3 cup of salmon.
4. Lift the edges to allow the uncooked portion to flow underneath them while the eggs set. Cook until the eggs are almost set.
5. Broil 6 inches from the heat source until the eggs are set completely, or for 1-2 minutes.
6. Fold the omelet in half and place onto a plate. Add a dill sprig and 2 tablespoons of creme fraiche on top.
7. Repeat the process for the remaining omelets.

Smoked Mushroom Salmon Tarts

Ingredients

- 4 cups sliced fresh mushrooms
- 2/3 cup smoked salmon or lox
- 1/3 cup crumbled feta cheese
- 8 large eggs, divided use
- 1 x 14.1 ounces package refrigerated pie pastry
- 1 tablespoon olive oil
- 1 medium red onion, thinly sliced
- 1 tablespoon butter
- 4 teaspoons drained capers, divided
- ½ teaspoon salt, divided
- ½ teaspoon pepper, divided
- 2 teaspoons snipped fresh dill, divided

Procedure

1. In 2 x 9 inches fluted tart pans that comes with removable bottoms, unroll pastry sheets; trim off all edges.
2. Keep in refrigerator for 30 minutes and set the oven to 400° and start preheating.
3. Line two layers of foil on an unpricked pastry. Fill with uncooked rice, dried beans or pie weights.
4. Arrange on a lower oven rack and bake for 10 to 15 minutes or until the color of edges turn to golden brown.
5. Remove weights and foil and bake for another 2 to 4 minutes or until the color of the bottom turn to golden brown.
6. Arrange on a wire rack to cool. Lower the oven heat to 375°.
7. Heat oil in a big skillet over medium high heat. Add onion and cook for 5 to 7 minutes or until light brown in color and softened, remember to stir while cooking.

8. Remove from pan. Add mushrooms and butter and cook for 6 to 8 minutes or until mushrooms are softened, remember to stir while cooking. Cool slightly.

9. Place each tart pan on a separate baking sheets. Distribute mushrooms and onion evenly between crusts; add cheese and salmon on top.

10. In a bowl, whisk together 1/4 teaspoon of each pepper and salt (optional), 2 teaspoons of capers and 4 eggs, stir in 1 teaspoon of dill.

11. Pour mixture over one of the tarts, repeat the same process for remaining ingredients, pour over the second tart.

12. Bake for 15 to 20 minutes or until a knife is still clean after being inserted into the center.

13. Allow to stand for 5 minutes prior to cutting.

Eggplant Eggs Benedict

Ingredients

- 8 x 1 inch thick slices eggplant
- 1 teaspoon white vinegar
- 8 large eggs
- 2 tablespoons olive oil
- 1/4 teaspoon salt
- 1/4 teaspoon white pepper
- 4 English muffins, split and toasted
- 8 ounces smoked salmon fillet, flaked
- ½ cup sour cream

For the Hollandaise Sauce:

- 3/4 cup butter, melted
- 1 teaspoon salt
- 1 large egg yolks
- 1/4 cup water
- 2 tablespoons lemon juice
- 1/4 teaspoon white pepper
- 2 tablespoons minced chives

Procedure

1. In a small bowl, mix pepper, salt and oil; brush over both sides of eggplant. Transfer to an ungreased 15x10x1-in. baking pan.
2. Broil 4-6 in. from the heat for 5-7 minutes on each side or until it is lightly browned and tender.
3. In the meantime, in a large skillet with high sides, pour 2-3 in. of water; add vinegar. Bring to a boil; lower the heat and gently simmer.
4. Break cold egg, one at a time, into a saucer or custard cup; keeping the cup near to the water's surface, slip each egg into water.
5. Cook without a cover until whites set completely and yolks start to get thick (but are not hard), about 4 minutes. Using a slotted spoon, remove each egg from the water.
6. Put 1 tablespoon sour cream, 3 tablespoons salmon, egg and an eggplant slice over each muffin half. Put aside and keep them warm.

7. Beat lemon juice, water and egg yolks constantly in a double boiler over simmering water until the mixture begins to thicken and covers the back of a metal spoon. Lower the heat to low. Drizzle slowly in melted butter, whipping constantly. Beat in salt and pepper.

8. Scoop 3 tablespoons sauce onto 8 serving plates. Put the prepared muffin and top with chives.

Salmon Stew

Ingredients

- 3 cups salmon broth
- 28 oz Crushed tomatoes
- 1 tsp Dried basil
- 1 tsp Dried oregano
- 2 cloves Garlic
- 0.5 tsp Black pepper
- 0.5 tsp Salt
- 8 oz Medium
- 6 oz salmon filets
- 2 stalks Celery
- 1 Red bell pepper
- 1 Onion
- 1 Tbsp Olive oil

Procedure

1. Dice/mince the garlic, celery, onions, and peppers.
2. Prepare an over-sized pot or dutch oven using the medium temperature setting to warm the oil.
3. Sauté the garlic, bell pepper, onion, celery, basil, and oregano until the onion is softened and translucent.
4. Stir in the crushed tomatoes and broth, bring to a simmer, and simmer until vegetables are soft, about 10 minutes.
5. Stir in the salmon and simmer until is cooked, about 5 minutes.

Spicy Salmon Dip

Ingredients

- ½ teaspoon salt
- 1 tablespoon minced chives
- 5 tablespoons butter
- ½ serrano chili, seeded and minced
- ½ teaspoon grated lemon zest
- 8 ounces salmon, cleaned and chopped
- Salt and freshly ground black pepper

Procedure

1. In a moderate-sized-sized sauté pan, melt the butter on moderate heat.
2. Mix in the chives, salt, chili pepper, and lemon zest; sauté for a couple of minutes.
3. Lower the heat to low and put in the salmon; sauté for about three minutes or until opaque.
4. Move the mixture to a food processor and crudely purée. Sprinkle with salt and pepper.
5. Firmly pack the purée into a small container. Cover using plastic wrap, and place in your fridge for 4 hours or overnight.
6. To serve, remove the salmon dip from the fridge and let it sit for five to ten minutes.
7. Serve the dip with an assortment of crackers and toast points or some favorite veggies.

Roasted Salmon

Ingredients

- ½ teaspoon sugar
- 1 tablespoon extra-virgin olive oil
- 12 ounces skinless salmon fillets, 1 inch thick
- 4 Lemon wedges
- Salt and pepper

Procedure

1. Place the oven rack in the center of the oven and pre-heat your oven to 425 degrees.
2. Pat salmon dry using paper towels, sprinkle with salt and pepper, and drizzle sugar uniformly 1 side of each fillet.
3. Heat oil in 12-inch oven-safe frying pan on moderate to high heat until just smoking.
4. Place salmon sugared side down in frying pan and press lightly to ensure even contact with skillet.
5. Cook until browned on first side, approximately two minutes.
6. Gently flip salmon using 2 spatulas, move frying pan to oven, and roast until fish flakes apart when softly poked using paring knife and registers 140 degrees, 7 to 10 minutes.
7. Serve with lemon wedges.

Salmon Patè

Ingredients

- 1 teaspoon sugar
- 2 cups minced salmon
- 2 tablespoons vegetable oil
- 1/4 teaspoon white pepper
- ½ teaspoon salt
- 1 red chili, seeded and thoroughly minced
- 8 pieces sugarcane

Procedure

1. Preheat your oven to 375 degrees.
2. Put the salmon, salt, sugar, white pepper, and chili in a food processor; process until the desired smoothness is achieved.
3. Sprinkle in one to 2 tablespoons of the vegetable oil. Process the salmon mixture until it reaches the consistency necessary to make a meatball, using nearly oil.
4. Split the salmon mixture into 4 equivalent portions.
5. Use your hands to mold a "salmon ball" around the center of each of the sugarcane pieces.
6. Put the "skewers" on a baking sheet and roast for roughly twenty minutes.
7. If you prefer them a little extra browned, broil them (after they are done baking) until the desired color is reached.
8. To serve, spoon some of the sweet-and-sour sauce into the middle of 4 plates.
9. Put the sugarcane "skewer" on top of the sauce.

Roasted Squash and Wild Salmon Risotto

Ingredients

- 4 roasted salmon fillets
- Salt and freshly ground black pepper
- 1 onion, peeled and chopped
- $^1/_3$ mug of grated Parmesan cheese
- A couple handfuls of rocket leaves, chopped
- 1 mug of risotto rice
- 2 mugs of butternut squash, peeled and diced into ½ inches cubes
- 1 mug Olive oil
- ½ mug of white wine
- 2 mugs of simmering chicken or vegetable stock
- 2 tbsp double cream

Procedure

1   Toss the diced squash in a little olive oil, season well with salt and pepper and place on a baking tray. Pop into a 375°F gas 5 oven for 20 minutes or so, turning occasionally. Remove from the oven just when the outer edges start to brown off.

2   Set aside to cool down and keep your picking fingers away from them, otherwise you won't have any to put into the risotto.

3   While they are cooling, sauté the onion with a glug of olive oil in a large heavy-based pot over a medium heat for 3–5 minutes.

4   Add the rice and wine and slowly simmer until the wine has almost evaporated, stirring constantly.

5   Now you start adding the stock to the rice a little at a time – as with the wine, you need to stir constantly and only add stock when the rice starts to thicken and get sticky. Keep the stock simmering in a separate saucepan.

6   Continue doing this until the rice is cooked through and your arm is about to fall off.

7 Finally, when the rice is cooked through, add the cream and half the Parmesan, stir through the rocket and baked squash, season and remove from the heat when the risotto is nice and sticky.

8 Sprinkle the remaining Parmesan and roasted salmon over each dish and serve.

Salmon in Mustard Sauce

Serves 4 pax

Ingredients

- ½ cup Fish Stock or Vegetable Stock
- 3/4 teaspoon kosher salt
- 2 tablespoons Dijon mustard
- 2 tablespoons vegetable oil
- 2 tablespoons unsalted butter
- 1/4 cup heavy cream
- ½ cup dry white wine
- All-purpose flour, for dredging
- 4 x 6-ounce skinless salmon fillets
- Freshly ground black pepper to taste

Procedure

1. Flavor the salmon fillets on both sides with 1/2teaspoon of the salt and some pepper. Heat a big nonstick frying pan on moderate to high heat.

2. Put in the vegetable oil. While the oil heats, spread the flour on a plate and gently dredge the salmon in it, patting off the surplus. Lightly put in the fillets to the frying pan.

3. Cook, flipping over once, until they are browned on both sides but not thoroughly cooked, approximately two minutes per side. Remove them to a plate.

4. Pour the surplus oil from the frying pan and wipe it clean using a paper towel. Melt the butter in the frying pan on moderate heat.

5. Put in the wine and bring to a simmer. Put in the fish stock and cream, and flavor with the rest of the 1/4 teaspoon salt.

6. Simmer, whisking once in a while, until the sauce is a little thickened, approximately 4 minutes.

7. Whisk in the mustard. Put in the salmon, flesh side up, and simmer, once in a while spooning the sauce over the salmon, until the fish is just thoroughly cooked—about three minutes, depending on the thickness of the salmon.

8. Serve instantly.

Stuffed Salmon

Ingredients

- 1 red bell pepper, stemmed, seeded, and chopped fine
- 1 red onion, chopped fine
- 1 tablespoon minced fresh parsley
- 1/3 cup pitted brine-cured green olives, chopped
- 10 ounces whole salmon, gutted
- 4 Lemon wedges
- Salt and pepper
- ½ preserved lemon, pulp and white pith removed, rind rinsed and minced
- 3 tablespoons extra-virgin olive oil

Procedure

1 Place the oven rack in the center of the oven and pre-heat your oven to 500 degrees.
2 Heat 2 tablespoons oil in 12-inch frying pan on moderate to high heat until it starts to shimmer.
3 Put in bell pepper and onion and cook until vegetables are softened and well browned, eight to ten minutes.
4 Mix in preserved lemon and cook until aromatic, approximately half a minute.
5 Remove from the heat, mix in olives and parsley and sprinkle with salt and pepper to taste.
6 Grease rimmed baking sheet with remaining 1 tablespoon oil. Wash each mackerel under cold running water and pat dry using paper towels inside and out.
7 Open cavity of each salmon, season flesh with salt and pepper, and spoon 1/4 of filling into opening.

8　Place salmon on readied sheet, spaced at least 2 inches apart. Bake until thickest part of salmon registers 130 to 135 degrees, 10 to 12 minutes.

9　Cautiously move salmon to serving platter and allow to rest for about five minutes.

10　Serve with lemon wedges.

Delicious Shrimp Recipes

Gain creativity, tastefulness and a fast weight-loss with these delicious, quick and easy recipes. Balance your proteins supply and learn new mouth-watering creations, thought to improve your skills and amaze your parties

Ernest Pescara

Shrimp Recipes

Pan-Fried Shrimps

Ingredients

- 1/2 teaspoon cayenne pepper, or to taste
- 1/2 teaspoon salt, or to taste
- 1 tablespoon vegetable oil
- 1/4 teaspoon crudely ground black pepper, or to taste
- 2 tablespoons Basic Ginger-Garlic Paste
- 2 tablespoons fresh lime juice
- 1/2 teaspoon crudely ground ajwain seeds
- 20 fresh or frozen (thawed) jumbo shrimp (11 to fifteen per pound), shelled and deveined, with tails intact
- 2 cups shredded lettuce, such as green or red leaf
- 5 Lime wedges

Procedure

1. Ready the ginger-garlic paste. Next, place the shrimp in a big non-reactive container.
2. Add all the rest of the ingredients (except the lettuce and lime wedges) and mix thoroughly, ensuring all the shrimp are coated thoroughly with the marinade.
3. Cover using plastic wrap and marinate in the fridge one to four hours.
4. Heat a non-stick skillet over medium high heat. Move the shrimp, one by one, to the skillet and cook, turning as required, until pink and opaque, 6 to 8 minutes.
5. Line a platter with shredded lettuce, move the shrimp to the platter before you serve with lime wedges on the side.

Sesamed Shrimps

Serves 5 pax

Ingredients

- 1 tablespoon Basic Ginger-Garlic Paste
- 1 tablespoon fresh lemon juice
- 1/4 teaspoon crudely ground ajwain seeds
- 1/2 teaspoon salt, or to taste
- 1 tablespoon Asian sesame oil
- 1 tablespoon white sesame seeds, crudely ground
- 1 teaspoon garam masala
- 2 teaspoons white sesame seeds, dry-roasted
- 3 scallions, green parts only, finely chopped
- 2 tablespoons non-fat plain yogurt, whisked until the desired smoothness is achieved
- 1 teaspoon ground dried fenugreek leaves
- 2 green chile peppers, such as serrano, thinly chopped on the diagonal
- 16 to 20 fresh jumbo shrimp (11 to fifteen per pound), shelled and deveined, with tails intact
- 2 small firm tomatoes, cut into 6 wedges each

Procedure

1. Roast the sesame seeds and ready the ginger-garlic paste. In each shrimp, make a slit by running the tip of a knife along the back curve, then opening them a bit, taking care that you do not cut right through.
2. In a large non-reactive container, combine the yogurt, sesame oil, lemon juice, ginger-garlic paste, sesame seeds, garam masala, fenugreek leaves, ajwain seeds, and salt.
3. Put in the shrimp and mix thoroughly, ensuring all the shrimp are coated thoroughly with the mixture. Cover using plastic wrap and marinate the shrimp at least 1 and maximum one day in a fridge.
4. Heat a large non-stick skillet using moderate to high heat. Next, with a slotted spoon, move each shrimp to the skillet, leaving behind the marinade, and cook, pressing softly using a spatula to flatten them.
5. Turn as required until the shrimp are golden on both sides and opaque, three to five minutes. Another way is to thread on metal skewers (or wood skewers soaked in water 30 minutes) and grill on a medium-hot (375°F to 400°F) grill until a golden colour is achieved. Move to a serving platter.
6. In the same skillet, lightly cook the tomatoes, stirring lightly and swaying the pan, until just softened, approximately half a minute. Put in the green chile peppers and scallions and stir approximately one minute. Scatter over the shrimp as a decoration.
7. Top with the dry-roasted sesame seeds and serve hot.

Spicy Grilled Shrimps

Serves 5 pax

Ingredients

- 16 to 20 fresh jumbo shrimp (11 to fifteen per pound), shelled and deveined, with tails intact
- 2 cups shredded lettuce, such as green or red leaf
- 2 tablespoons fresh lemon juice
- 5 metal skewers or wooden skewers soaked in water 30 minutes
- 1/2 teaspoon salt, or to taste
- 2 tablespoons Gujarati Green Paste

Procedure

1. Ready the masala paste. Next, put the shrimp in a big non-reactive container.
2. Put in the masala paste, lemon juice, and salt and mix until all the shrimp are coated thoroughly with the marinade. Cover and marinate at least 2 and maximum one day in a fridge.
3. Preheat the grill to moderate-high (375°F to 400°F). Line a serving platter with the lettuce. Thread the shrimp on the skewers and grill 3 to four minutes per side, turning once, until mildly charred and opaque.
4. Move to the serving platter.
5. Serve hot.

Tangy Shrimps

Ingredients

- 1/4 teaspoon salt, or to taste
- 1 (1-inch) piece peeled fresh ginger, cut into thin matchsticks
- 1/4 cup minced fresh curry leaves
- 1/4 teaspoon ground turmeric
- 1 cup Coconut Milk
- 1 large tomato, finely chopped
- 1 tablespoon Basic Ginger-Garlic Paste
- 2 tablespoons Tamarind Paste
- 12 fresh curry leaves
- 1 tablespoon ground coriander
- 3 fresh green chile peppers, such as serrano, minced with seeds
- 16 to 20 fresh jumbo shrimp (11 to fifteen per pound), shelled and deveined, with tails intact
- 2 tablespoons coconut or vegetable oil
- 2 tablespoons minced fresh mint leaves

Procedure

1. Ready the ginger-garlic paste and the coconut milk. Rinse the kokum halves well, cut finely and soak the pieces in 1 cup hot water for approximately half an hour. Drain and reserve the water. Or combine the tamarind paste with 1 cup water.
2. Heat the oil in a big non-stick wok or saucepan using moderate to high heat and cook the ginger matchsticks until a golden color is achieved, approximately one minute.
3. Stir in the ginger-garlic paste, curry leaves, and green chile peppers and cook using moderate to low heat, stirring, approximately one minute.
4. Stir in the tomato, coriander, turmeric, soaked kokum pieces (or tamarind mixture), curry leaves, and salt, and stir approximately five minutes. Put in the shrimp and cook, flipping over once or twice, approximately one minute, then put in the reserved kokum water (if not using tamarind), and bring to a boil using high heat. Decrease the heat to moderate to low, cover the pan, and simmer until the shrimp are pink and opaque and the juices are almost dry, approximately seven minutes.
5. Stir in the coconut milk and cook approximately two minutes. Move to a serving dish, stir in the mint leaves before you serve.

Chile-Fried Shrimps

Serves 5 pax

Ingredients

- 1 large onion, finely chopped
- 1 large tomato, finely chopped
- 1 small green bell pepper, cut into 1/2-inch pieces
- 1 teaspoon ground cumin
- 1/4 teaspoon ground turmeric
- 1/2 teaspoon garam masala
- 1/2 teaspoon hot red pepper flakes, or to taste
- 3 fresh green chile peppers, minced with seeds
- 2 tablespoons fresh lime juice, or more to taste
- 2 tablespoons minced fresh curry leaves
- 2 tablespoons ground coriander
- 16 to 20 fresh jumbo shrimp (11 to fifteen per pound), shelled and deveined, with tails intact
- 2 tablespoons Basic Ginger-Garlic Paste
- 2 tablespoons coconut or peanut oil
- 2 tablespoons finely chopped fresh cilantro

Procedure

1. Ready the ginger-garlic paste. Put the shrimp in a medium non-reactive container, add 1 tablespoon ginger-garlic paste, the hot pepper flakes, coriander, turmeric, and 1 tablespoon curry leaves and mix thoroughly.
2. Cover using plastic wrap and marinate the shrimp at least 1 and maximum one day in a fridge.
3. Heat the oil in a big non-stick wok or saucepan using moderate to high heat and cook the onion, stirring, until a golden color is achieved, approximately five minutes.
4. Stir in the rest of the ginger-garlic paste, the green chile peppers, and the rest of the curry leaves and cook, continuing to stir, approximately one minute.
5. Put in the garam masala and cumin, then stir in the tomato and bell pepper and cook until all the liquids vaporize and the bell pepper is soft, approximately five minutes.
6. Put in the marinated shrimp plus the marinade, and cook, stirring, until the shrimp are pink and opaque, approximately seven minutes.
7. Stir in the lemon juice and cilantro. Move to a serving dish and serve hot.

Marinated Shrimps and Bell Peppers

Ingredients

- 1/2 teaspoon ajwain seeds
- 1 cup crudely chopped fresh cilantro
- 1/4 teaspoon cayenne pepper, or to taste
- 1/4 teaspoon garam masala
- 1 cup canned tomato sauce
- 1 large green mango, peeled and cut into 1/2-inch pieces
- 1 small onion, crudely chopped
- 1 tablespoon ground coriander
- 2 small onions, cut in half along the length and thinly chopped
- 2 tablespoons vegetable oil
- 3 quarter-size slices peeled fresh ginger
- 1 teaspoon dried fenugreek leaves
- 1 teaspoon salt, or to taste
- 16 to 20 fresh jumbo shrimp (11 to fifteen per pound), shelled and deveined, with tails intact
- 1 large clove fresh garlic, peeled
- 2 small bell peppers (1 red, 1 yellow), finely chopped

Procedure

1. Using a food processor or blender, combine and pulse 1/4 cup mango, onion, ginger, garlic, and 1/2 cup cilantro until a smooth paste is achieved. Put in the ajwain seeds, cayenne pepper, and 1/4 teaspoon salt and process once more.
2. Put the shrimp in a non-reactive container. Put in the processed paste and mix thoroughly, ensuring all the pieces are coated thoroughly with the marinade. Cover using plastic wrap and marinate in the fridge for minimum 1 and maximum one day.
3. In the meantime, heat 2 tablespoons oil in a big non-stick wok or saucepan and cook the onions, stirring, until a golden color is achieved, approximately five minutes. Put in the bell peppers and the rest of the mango and stir approximately three minutes.
4. Put in the coriander, fenugreek leaves, and the rest of the salt, stir in the canned tomato sauce and cook, stirring, approximately two minutes. Turn off the heat.
5. Heat the rest of the 1 tablespoon oil in a big non-stick skillet using moderate to high heat and cook the shrimp plus the marinade, stirring, until the shrimp are pink and opaque and almost dry, approximately seven minutes.
6. Combine with the sauce, put in the rest of the 1/2 cup cilantro, and cook another two minutes to blend the flavors.
7. Move to a serving dish, sprinkle the garam masala on top before you serve hot.

Sautéed Shrimps with Garlic

Ingredients

- Salt and fresh ground black pepper
- 2 garlic cloves, chopped fine
- 2 tablespoons capers, drained
- 1/4 cup extra-virgin olive oil
- 2 pounds fresh shrimp, peeled and deveined
- 1/4 cup fresh squeezed lemon juice
- 2 tablespoons parsley

Procedure

1. Season shrimp with salt and pepper to taste.
2. Heat 2 tablespoons olive oil in large skillet. When oil shimmers, add seasoned shrimp. Sauté 2 minutes on high heat.
3. When lightly brown and turning opaque, add remainder of olive oil, garlic and capers. Sauté 30 seconds.
4. Flip shrimp over. Add lemon juice and half the parsley. Cover and cook 5 minutes on low heat Shrimp are done when cooked through.
5. Transfer shrimp to plates.
6. Spoon the Provençal sauce from skillet over shrimp.
7. Sprinkle remaining parsley on top.

Shrimp Bisque

Ingredients

- 1/2 onion, minced
- 1 bay leaf
- 1/8 teaspoon thyme
- 1/4 cup butter
- 8 ounces shrimp, peeled and deveined
- 1 rib of celery, finely diced
- 1/4 cup sherry
- 1/2 cup flour
- 3 teaspoons paprika
- 2 cups fresh cream
- 1 teaspoon tomato paste
- 2 pinches fresh ground nutmeg
- 1 pinch of salt
- 1 cup milk

Procedure

1. Melt 1 tablespoon butter in skillet. Sauté shrimp until pink. Remove and set aside shrimp.
2. Add 1 tablespoon butter to skillet. Sauté celery and onion 7 minutes. When vegetables are soft, add bay leaf, thyme and sherry. Cook 2 minutes. Remove bay leaf.
3. Purée remaining mixture. Melt remaining butter in saucepan. Add flour and stir 3 minutes on low heat.
4. When roux bubbles, stir in reserved purée. Add milk, paprika, nutmeg and salt. Cook on low heat.
5. Stir until slightly thickened. Reserve 4 shrimp for garnish. Chop remaining shrimp.
6. Add shrimp, tomato paste and cream to pan.
7. Heat thoroughly without boiling. When piping hot, pour bisque into 4 serving bowls.
8. Garnish each bowl with a shrimp.
9. Serve immediately with sourdough croutons.

Shrimp Lettuce Wraps

Serves 7 pax

Ingredients

- 1 Tbsp Peanut butter
- 0.25 cups chicken broth
- 1 Lime zest and juice
- 0.5 large Avocado
- 7 large leaves Boston lettuce
- 1 Tbsp Chives
- 1 clove Garlic
- 1 tsp Fresh ginger
- 1 small Onion
- 1 bell pepper
- 1 tsp Sesame oil
- 1 tsp Thai-style chili garlic paste
- 1 tsp Splenda brown sugar blend
- 1 Tbsp Soy sauce
- 9 lb Shrimp

Procedure

1. Stir together the soy sauce, Splenda, chili garlic paste, ginger, garlic, lime zest, lime juice, chicken broth, and peanut butter; set aside.
2. In a medium-sized nonstick skillet, warm the oil using the med-high temperature setting. Sauté the onion and bell pepper until softened, and the onions are translucent.
3. Add the shrimp and cook (2-3 min.). Mix in the sauce mixture and simmer until the shrimp is fully cooked and the sauce has thickened. Stir in the chives.
4. Place 0.25 cups of the shrimp mixture on each lettuce leaf and top with avocado.
5. Serve.

Greek-Style Shrimp

Serves 5 pax

Ingredients

- 1 (28-ounce) can diced tomatoes
- 1 red or green bell pepper, seeded, and chopped
- 1 small onion, chopped
- 1/4 cup dry white wine
- 1/4 cup extra-virgin olive oil
- 1/2 teaspoon red pepper flakes
- 1 teaspoon grated lemon zest
- 3 tablespoons coarsely chopped fresh parsley
- 4 tablespoons ouzo
- 2 garlic cloves, minced
- 2 pounds extra-large shrimp (21 to 25 per pound), peeled and deveined
- 3 tablespoons chopped fresh dill
- 2 ounces feta cheese, crumbled
- Salt and pepper

Procedure

1. Toss shrimp in a container with 1 tablespoon oil, 1 tablespoon ouzo, 1 teaspoon garlic, lemon zest, 1/4 teaspoon salt, and 1/8 teaspoon pepper; set aside.

2. Heat 2 tablespoons oil in 12-inch frying pan on moderate heat until it starts to shimmer. Put in onion, bell pepper, and 1/4 teaspoon salt, cover, and cook, stirring intermittently, until vegetables release their liquid, 3 to 5 minutes.

3. Uncover and continue to cook, stirring intermittently, until liquid evaporates and vegetables are softened, approximately five minutes. Mix in remaining garlic and pepper flakes and cook until aromatic, approximately one minute.

4. Mix in tomatoes and reserved juice, wine, and remaining 2 tablespoons ouzo. Bring to simmer and cook, stirring intermittently, until flavors blend and sauce is slightly thickened (sauce should not be completely dry), five to ten minutes. Mix in parsley and sprinkle with salt and pepper to taste.

5. Decrease heat to moderate to low and put in shrimp along with any accumulated juices; stir to coat and distribute evenly.

6. Cover and cook, stirring intermittently, until shrimp are opaque throughout, 6 to 9 minutes, adjusting heat as required to maintain bare simmer.

7. Remove from the heat, drizzle with feta and dill and drizzle with remaining 1 tablespoon oil.

8. Serve.

Italian Shrimp & White Beans

Ingredients

- 1 red bell pepper, stemmed, seeded, and chopped
- 1 small red onion, chopped fine
- 1/4 teaspoon red pepper flakes
- 1 pound extra-large shrimp (21 to 25 per pound), peeled and deveined
- 2 (15-ounce) cans cannellini beans, rinsed
- Pinch sugar
- Salt and pepper
- 2 garlic cloves, minced
- 2 ounces baby arugula, chopped coarse
- 2 tablespoons lemon juice
- 5 tablespoons extra-virgin olive oil

Procedure

1. Pat shrimp dry using paper towels and season with sugar, salt, and pepper. Heat 1 tablespoon oil in 12-inch non-stick frying pan on high heat until just smoking.
2. Put in shrimp to frying pan in one layer and cook, without stirring, until spotty brown and edges turn pink on first side, approximately one minute.
3. Remove from the heat, flip shrimp and allow to sit until opaque throughout, approximately half a minute. Move shrimp to a container and cover to keep warm.
4. Heat remaining 1/4 cup oil in now-empty frying pan on moderate heat until it starts to shimmer. Put in bell pepper, onion, and 1/2 teaspoon salt and cook till they become tender, approximately five minutes.
5. Mix in garlic and pepper flakes and cook until aromatic, approximately half a minute. Mix in beans and cook until heated through, approximately five minutes.

6. Put in arugula and shrimp along with any accumulated juices and gently toss until arugula is wilted, approximately one minute.
7. Mix in lemon juice and sprinkle with salt and pepper to taste.
8. Serve.

Moroccan Shrimp Skewers

Ingredients

For the Marinade:

- 1/4 teaspoon cayenne pepper
- 1 teaspoon grated lime zest
- 3 tablespoons extra-virgin olive oil
- 6 garlic cloves, minced
- 1/2 teaspoon ground cumin
- 1/2 teaspoon ground ginger
- 1/2 teaspoon salt
- 1/2 teaspoon smoked paprika

For the Shrimps:

- 1 Tablespoon Minced Fresh Cilantro
- 1/2 Teaspoon Sugar
- 2 pounds extra-large shrimp (21 to 25 per pound), peeled and deveined
- Lime Wedges

Procedure

For the Marinade:

1. Beat all ingredients together in medium bowl.

For the Shrimps:

2. Pat shrimp dry using paper towels. Using sharp paring knife, make shallow cut down outside curve of shrimp.
3. Put in shrimp to a container with marinade and toss to coat. Cover and put in the fridge for minimum half an hour or maximum 1 hour.
4. On a gas grill, turn all burners to high, cover, and heat grill until hot, about fifteen minutes.
5. Leave all burners on high.
6. Clean and oil cooking grate. Thread shrimp tightly onto four 12-inch metal skewers (about 12 shrimp per skewer), alternating direction of heads and tails.
7. Sprinkle 1 side of skewered shrimp with sugar. Place shrimp skewers sugared side down on grill (on hotter side if using charcoal).
8. Cook (covered if using gas), without moving them, until mildly charred on first side, three to five minutes. Flip skewers and move to cooler side of grill (if using charcoal) or turn all burners off (if using gas) and cook, covered, until shrimp are opaque throughout, 1 to 2 minutes.
9. Using tongs, slide shrimp off skewers onto serving platter and sprinkle with salt and pepper to taste.
10. Sprinkle with cilantro and serve with lime wedges.

Shrimp Fritters

Serves 24 botanas

Ingredients

- 1/2 cup finely chopped white onion
- 1 cup cold water
- 1 egg white
- 3/4 cup small dried shrimps, cleaned
- 2 ounces flour
- 2 serrano chiles, finely chopped
- Salt to taste
- Vegetable oil for frying

Procedure

1. Combine the flour, water, and salt together for a couple of minutes and leave the batter to stand for minimum 1 hour.
2. Wash the shrimps to remove surplus salt. Cover with warm water and leave them to soak for approximately five minutes—no longer.
3. Beat the egg white until stiff and fold it into the batter.
4. Drain the shrimps (if large, cut into 2) and put in them, with the chopped onion and chiles, to the batter.
5. Heat the oil in a frying pan and drop tablespoons of the mixture into it, a few at a time. Fry the botanas until they become golden brown, flipping them over once.
6. Drain them on the paper towelling and serve instantly.

Tequila Lime Shrimp Noodles

Serves 4 pax

Ingredients

- 2 Tbsp Lime juice
- 1.5 tsp Lime zest
- 5 Tbsp Olive oil
- 1 Tbsp Butter
- 1 cup Tequila
- 1 lb Uncooked shrimp
- 2 Zucchini
- 1 Tbsp Fresh parsley
- 2 Garlic cloves
- quarter tsp Pepper
- half tsp Salt
- 1 Shallot

Procedure

1. Place a big skillet onto a burner on a medium setting and melt two Tbsp. of butter.
2. Add in your garlic and shallot and let them cook for two minutes. Take the skillet away from heat and mix in the tequila, lime zest, and juice.
3. Put the pan back on the burner and cook to reduce the liquid until the liquid is almost all gone.
4. Pour in the olive oil and remaining butter. Mix in the shrimp and zucchini.
5. Add your salt and pepper and cook until the shrimp begins to turn pink and the zucchini begins to tenderize.
6. Sprinkle fresh parsley over the mixture and add additional lime zest if you choose to.

Shrimp and Rice

Ingredients

- 3/4 cup finely chopped white onion
- 1 cup fruity (but not extra virgin) olive oil
- 1 small red bell pepper, thinly cut
- 1 teaspoon dried mexican oregano
- 2 cups long-grain unconverted white rice, washed and drained
- 2 pounds medium shrimps, unshelled
- 12 ounces tomatoes, finely chopped
- 2 garlic cloves, finely chopped
- 2 heaped tablespoons roughly chopped cilantro
- 2 tablespoons roughly chopped chives
- 2 tablespoons roughly chopped mint
- 5 cups water or fish broth
- Salt to taste

Procedure

1. Heat the olive oil in a deep—about 5 inches (13 cm) deep—flameproof casserole. Put in the shrimps and a good drizzle of salt, and stir-fry using high heat for approximately one minute.

2. Remove using a slotted spoon and save for later. In the same oil fry the tomatoes, onion, pepper, and garlic on moderate heat until well amalgamated— about five minutes.

3. Mix in the rice, put in the water with salt to taste, and bring to its boiling point. Cover the pan and cook on moderate heat for approximately 8 minutes.

4. Put in the shrimps and herbs and carry on cooking, covered, still on moderate heat, until the rice is soft —about ten minutes.

5. The consistency must be soupy.

South Guaca Shrimps

Ingredients

- 1 pound tomatoes, cored, seeded, and slice into 1/2 inch pieces
- 1 tablespoon lime juice, plus lime wedges for serving
- 1/8 teaspoon sugar
- 1/4 cup minced fresh cilantro
- 1 avocado, halved, pitted, and diced
- 2 pounds extra big shrimp (21 to 25 per pound), peeled and deveined
- 2 garlic cloves, minced
- 2 scallions, white and green parts separated and cut
- Salt and pepper
- 2 teaspoons minced canned chipotle chile in adobo sauce
- 2 tablespoons vegetable oil

Procedure

1. Toss tomatoes, scallion whites, cilantro, garlic, chipotle, and 3/4 teaspoon salt together in container. In separate container, toss shrimp with sugar, 1/4 teaspoon salt, and 1/4 teaspoon pepper.
2. Heat 1 tablespoon oil in 12 inches frying pan using high heat until just smoking. Put in half of shrimp to pan in single layer and cook, without moving, until spotty brown on one side, approximately one minute.
3. Move shrimp to big container (they will be underdone). Repeat with remaining 1 tablespoon oil and shrimp.
4. Return now empty frying pan to high heat, put in tomato mixture and lime juice, and cook until tomatoes are slightly softened, approximately one minute.
5. Mix in shrimp with any collected juices and cook until shrimp are thoroughly cooked and hot, approximately one minute.
6. Move shrimp to big platter and drizzle with avocado and scallion greens. Serve with lime wedges.

Basil Shrimp

Ingredients

- 1/2 cup julienned basil
- tablespoons water
- 4 eggs
- Salt and pepper to taste
- 1/2 pound cooked salad shrimp
- 1 green onion, trimmed and thinly cut
- 1 teaspoon fish sauce
- 2 teaspoons vegetable oil, divided

Procedure

1. Put 1 teaspoon of the vegetable oil in a sauté pan on moderate heat. Put in the shrimp and green onion, and sauté until the shrimp are warmed through, roughly two minutes.
2. Put in the basil and fish sauce and cook for 1 more minute. Set aside.
3. In a big container, whisk together the eggs, water, and salt and pepper, then mix in the shrimp mixture.
4. Put the remaining 1/2 teaspoon of vegetable oil in an omelet pan on moderate heat. Put in the egg mixture and cook until the omelet starts to brown. Turn over the omelet and carry on cooking until set.
5. To serve, slide the omelet onto a serving plate and cut it into wedges.
6. Serve with a Thai dipping sauce of your choice.

Shrimp Bisque with Corn Custard

Ingredients

- 2 tablespoons tomato purée
- 1 sprig of fresh parsley
- 3/4 pints fish stock
- 6 ounces butter
- 1 ounce flour
- salt and pepper
- 8 pounds whole shrimp, peeled
- 1 bay leaf
- 1 small onion, skinned
- 1 small carrot, peeled
- 4 tablespoons single cream
- 4 tablespoons brandy

Procedure

1. Dice the carrot and chop up the onion. Place in pan with the bay leaf, parsley, tomato purée and fish stock. Bring to a boil, cover and then simmer for 30 minutes.
2. Filter mixture through a sieve to smooth it and return pan after rinsing. Mix the butter with the flour until evenly blended and creamy.
3. Add to the soup in small dollops one at a time. Bring to a boil over moderate heat stirring continually. Lower to a simmer and stir for 2 minutes until thick and smooth.
4. Hold a few shrimps back for garnish and stir the remainder into the bisque. Add brandy and cream, then heat and stir gently for one minute. Season to taste with salt and pepper.
5. Serve into pre-warmed soup dishes.
6. Float the garnish shrimps on top of the bisque and serve hot.

Singapore Shrimps

Ingredients

- 1 clove garlic, minced
- 1 cup cut domestic mushrooms
- 1 teaspoon minced ginger
- 2 pounds cooked shrimp
- 4 tablespoons vegetable oil
- 1/4 cup green onion slices
- 1/4 teaspoon Chinese 5-spice powder
- 1 coconut milk
- 3 teaspoons hoisin sauce
- 3 teaspoons oyster sauce
- 2 teaspoons Red Curry Paste
- Salt and pepper

Procedure

1. In a wok or big sauté pan, heat the vegetable oil on moderate to high.
2. Put in the mushrooms, green onions, garlic, and ginger; stir-fry for two to three
3. minutes.
4. Mix together the hoisin sauce, oyster sauce, and curry paste, and 5-spice powder until well blended. Put in the mixture to the wok.
5. Mix in the coconut milk and tweak seasoning to taste with the salt and pepper. Put in the shrimp and bring to a simmer.
6. Cook for one to two minutes until the shrimp are thoroughly heated.

Roasted Garlic Shrimp

Serves 6 pax

Ingredients

- 1/4 teaspoon pepper
- 1/2 teaspoon red pepper flakes
- 1 teaspoon anise seeds
- 10 pounds shell-on jumbo shrimp
- 1/4 cup extra-virgin olive oil
- 1/4 cup salt
- 3 tablespoons minced fresh parsley
- 6 garlic cloves, minced
- Lemon wedges

Procedure

1. Dissolve salt in 4 cups cold water in large container. Using kitchen shears or sharp paring knife, cut through shell of shrimp and devein but do not remove shell. Use a paring knife to continue to cut shrimp 1/2 inch deep, taking care not to cut in half fully. Immerse shrimp in brine, cover, put inside your fridge for about fifteen minutes.

2. Place oven rack 4 inches from broiler element and heat broiler. Mix oil, garlic, anise seeds, pepper flakes, and pepper in a big container. Remove shrimp from brine and pat dry using paper towels. Put in shrimp and parsley to oil mixture and toss well, making sure oil mixture gets into interior of shrimp. Arrange shrimp in one layer on wire rack set in rimmed baking sheet.

3. Broil shrimp until opaque and shells are starting to brown, 2 to 4 minutes, rotating sheet halfway through broiling. Flip shrimp and continue to broil until second side is opaque and shells are starting to brown, 2 to 4 minutes, rotating sheet halfway through broiling. Serve with lemon wedges.

Bacon-Wrapped Shrimp

Serves 10 pax

Ingredients

- 4 large leaves Romaine lettuce
- 7 slices Bacon
- 20 raw Shrimps

Procedure

1. Wrap one piece of bacon around each shrimp. Place them on a baking sheet coated in nonstick spray. Try to get the ends of the bacon under the shrimp, but it's fine if you can't easily do that.
2. Place the baking sheet under a preheated broiler and broil for 2 to 3 minutes per side.
3. Arrange the shrimp on the lettuce leaves and serve. Store leftovers in the refrigerator in an airtight container.
4. This recipe is simple, but it's a crowd pleaser! That doesn't mean you need a crowd to enjoy this recipe full of lean protein, however; they are simple enough to make for any regular day.
5. Sprinkle the shrimp with any herbs and spice.

Shrimp Tacos Slaw

Serves 6 pax

Ingredients

- 1 pound jícama, peeled and slice into 3 inch long
- 1 tablespoon minced fresh oregano
- 1/4 cup thinly cut red onion
- 1 cup Mexican crema
- 1 teaspoon garlic powder
- 3 tablespoons chopped fresh cilantro
- 4 tablespoons vegetable oil
- 6 Lime wedges
- 1 teaspoon grated orange zest plus 1/3 cup juice
- 18 (6 inch) corn tortillas
- 2 pounds extra big shrimp (21 to 25 per pound), peeled, deveined, and tails removed
- 2 teaspoons chipotle chile powder
- Salt

Procedure

1. Mix jícama, orange zest and juice, onion, cilantro, and 1/2 teaspoon salt in container, cover, and place in your fridge until ready to serve.

2. Whisk oil, oregano, chile powder, garlic powder, and 1/2 teaspoon salt together in big container. Pat shrimp dry using paper towels, put into spice mixture, and toss to coat.

3. Thread shrimp onto four 12 inches metal skewers, alternating direction of heads and tails.

4. **For A Gas Grill:** Set all burners to high, cover, and heat grill until hot, approximately fifteen minutes. Leave all burners on high.

5. Clean and oil cooking grate. Put shrimp on grill and cook (covered if using gas) until mildlly charred on first side, approximately 4 minutes.

6. Flip shrimp, pushing them together on skewer if they separate, and cook until opaque throughout, approximately 2 minutes.

7. Move to platter and cover using aluminium foil.

8. Working in batches, grill tortillas, turning as required, until warm and soft, approximately half a minute; wrap firmly in foil to keep tender.
9. Slide shrimp off skewers onto cutting board and slice into 1/2 inch pieces.
10. Serve with tortillas, jícama slaw, crema, and lime wedges.

Tequila Sour Quesadillas

Ingredients

- 1 teaspoon grated lime zest
- 1 teaspoon minced canned chipotle chile in adobo sauce
- 2 pounds medium big shrimp (31 to 40 per pound), peeled, deveined, tails removed, and halved along the length
- 2 tablespoons vegetable oil
- 4 (10 inch) flour tortillas
- 1/4 cup minced fresh cilantro
- 1/3 cup tequila
- 12 ounces Monterey Jack cheese, shredded
- 2 garlic cloves, minced
- 2 scallions, white and green parts separated, cut
- Salt and pepper

Procedure

1. Adjust oven rack to middle position and heat oven to 450 degrees. Coat rimmed baking sheet with aluminium foil and brush with 1 tablespoon oil. Toss Monterey Jack with cilantro and scallion greens.
2. Pat dry shrimp using paper towels and sprinkle with salt and pepper. Heat 1
3. tablespoon oil in 12 inches nonstick frying pan on moderate heat until it starts to shimmer.
4. Put in scallion whites, garlic, chipotle, and 1/4 teaspoon salt and cook until tender, approximately 2 minutes.
5. Put in tequila amd simmer until tequila has vaporized and pan is dry, approximately five minutes.
6. Put in shrimp and cook, stirring frequently, until thoroughly cooked and opaque throughout, approximately 3 minutes.
7. Move to container, mix in zest, and allow to cool for five minutes; drain thoroughly.

8. Place tortillas on counter. Drizzle half of cheese mixture over half of each tortilla, leaving 1/2 inch border around edge.

9. Position shrimp on top in single layer, then drizzle with rest of the cheese mixture. Fold other half of each tortilla over top and press tightly to compact.

10. Position quesadillas in single layer on readied sheet with rounded edges facing center of sheet. Brush with remaining 1 tablespoon oil.

11. Bake until quesadillas start to brown, approximately ten minutes. Flip quesadillas over and push softly with spatula to compact.

12. Carry on baking until crunchy and golden brown on second side, approximately five minutes. Allow quesadillas to cool on wire rack for five minutes, then slice each into 4 wedges before you serve.

Curry Shrimps and Peas

Serves 6 pax

Ingredients

- 1 cup packed cilantro, chopped
- 1 tablespoon vegetable oil
- 2 teaspoons Red Curry Paste
- 9 pounds big shrimp, peeled and deveined
- 3 teaspoons brown sugar
- 10 ounces package thawed frozen peas
- 14 ounces unsweetened coconut milk
- 1 cup packed basil leaves, chopped
- 2 teaspoons fish sauce
- Jasmine rice, cooked in accordance with package

Procedure

1. In a big pot, mix the curry paste, vegetable oil, and 1/4 cup of the coconut milk; cook on moderate heat for one to two minutes.
2. Mix in the rest of the coconut milk and cook for an extra five minutes.
3. Put in the fish sauce and sugar and cook for a minute more.
4. Put in the shrimp, basil, and cilantro; decrease the heat slightly and cook for four to five minutes or until the shrimp are almost done.
5. Put in the peas and cook two minutes more.
6. Serve over Jasmine rice.

Shrimps Watercress Salad

Ingredients

- 2 large bunches of watercress (for the cooked one) or 1 large bunch (for the raw one)
- 2 cups peeled and steamed shrimps
- 1 tbsp soy sauce
- 2 tbsp sesame oil
- 3 tbsp Sesame seeds
- 1 tbsp rice wine vinegar

Procedure

1. Heat a frying pan over a low heat and add the sesame seeds (no oil needed).
2. In a couple of minutes, they will start to smell delicious and turn brown. When they do, tip them out of the pan so that they stop cooking. It's easy to burn the seeds, so watch them like a paranoid hawk and shake the pan about from time to time as they cook.
3. Next, blanch the watercress by pouring boiling water over it in a bowl and leaving it for about 30 seconds, then drain and squeeze out any excess water with your hands. Chop it coarsely. If you're using raw watercress, just jump straight to the coarse chopping bit.
4. Mix the dressing ingredients and the shrimps together well and pour over the watercress.
5. Sprinkle with sesame seeds and serve with some grilled fish and rice.

Sea Sausage

Serves 4 feet sausage

Ingredients

- 1 pound fish, cut in 1/2-inch slices, skin and bone removed and reserved
- 8 ounces raw shrimps, cleaned and deveined, shells reserved

For the broth:

- 1 celery rib, roughly chopped
- 1 tablespoon fresh lime juice
- 2 bay leaves, mexican if possible
- 2 sprigs fresh thyme
- 4 cups water
- 6 peppercorns
- 3 small carrots, scraped and cut
- 3 sprigs flat-leaf parsley
- 3 teaspoons salt, or to taste

For the sausage:

- 1/4 cup finely chopped white onion
- 2/3 cup peas

- 1 medium waxy potato, peeled, partly cooked
- 1 tablespoon fresh lime juice
- 1 teaspoon salt, or to taste
- 2 tablespoons finely chopped fresh parsley
- 1 jalapeño chile or any fresh, finely chopped
- 1 medium carrot, diced small, and partly cooked
- 4 feet sausage casings, roughly
- 6 ounces tomatoes, finely chopped
- 6 tablespoons olive oil, roughly
- Freshly ground black pepper

Procedure

1. Place the fish and shrimps into the freezer and leave for approximately 2 hours or until half frozen.

2. Prepare the broth. Place the debris from the fish and shrimps into a wide deep cooking pan, with the remaining broth ingredients. Bring to its boiling point and simmer for approximately forty minutes. Strain the broth and return to the deep cooking pan.

3. Place the fish and shrimps, a small quantity at a time to stop the blades from clogging, into a blender jar or food processor and grind until fine.

165

4. Combine the fish paste with the remaining sausage ingredients, using only 2 tablespoons of the oil.
5. Fry one spoonful of the mixture now for taste, then tweak the seasoning if required and stuff into the casing, using any standard stuffing method; make two lengths approximately 1 inch thick, then prick all over with a very sharp pointed fork.
6. Reheat the broth, and when it begins to simmer, put in the sausages in flat coils. The broth should completely cover the sausages; if it does not, then put in more hot water.
7. Heat to a simmer and cook for approximately fifteen to twenty minutes, then remove and drain. Let ripen in your fridge for a few days—this will improve the flavor—then proceed.
8. Chop the sausage into slices about 1/2 inch thick.
9. Heat the rest of the 4 tablespoons oil, then reduce the heat and fry the sausage slices until a golden-brown color is achieved.
10. Serve hot.

Shrimps, Garlic, Cilantro and Lime

Serves 5 pax

Ingredients

- 1/2 teaspoon red pepper flakes
- 1 teaspoon annatto powder
- 2 pounds shell on jumbo shrimp (16 to 20 per pound)
- 1/4 cup minced fresh cilantro
- 1/4 cup salt
- 1/2 cup vegetable oil
- 2 teaspoons coriander seeds, lightly crushed
- 2 teaspoons grated lime zest, plus lime wedges
- 6 garlic cloves, minced

Procedure

1. Dissolve salt in 1 quart cold water in big container. Using kitchen shears or sharp paring knife, cut through shells of shrimp and devein but do not remove shells.

2. Use a paring knife to continue to cut shrimp 1/2 inch deep, ensuring not to cut in half completely. Submerge shrimp in brine, cover, and place in your fridge for fifteen minutes.

3. Adjust oven rack 4 inches from broiler element and heat broiler. Set wire rack in rimmed baking sheet.

4. Mix oil, cilantro, garlic, coriander seeds, lime zest, annatto, and pepper flakes in big container. Remove shrimp from brine, pat dry using paper towels, and put into oil mixture.

5. Toss thoroughly, ensuring mixture gets into interior of shrimp. Position shrimp in single layer on prepared rack.

6. Broil shrimp until opaque and shells are starting to brown, 2 to 4 minutes, rotating sheet midway through broiling.
7. Flip shrimp and continue to broil until second side appears opaque and shells are starting to brown, 2 to 4 minutes, rotating sheet midway through broiling.
8. Move shrimp to serving platter and serve with lime wedges.

Spicy Shrimps

Ingredients

- 1 onion, chopped fine
- 1 tablespoon lime juice, plus wedges for serving
- 1 tablespoon minced chipotle chile in adobo sauce
- 1/4 cup chopped fresh cilantro or parsley
- 1 (8 ounce) can tomato sauce
- 2 garlic cloves, minced
- 2 dried guajillo chiles, stemmed, seeded and torn into 1/2 inch pieces
- Salt and pepper
- 1 cup water
- 2 pounds extra big shrimp (21 to 25 per pound), peeled and deveined
- 2 tablespoons extra virgin olive oil, plus for serving
- 2 teaspoons dried oregano

Procedure

1. Toast guajillo chiles in Dutch oven on moderate heat, stirring regularly, until aromatic, 2 to six minutes; move to container.
2. Heat oil in now empty pot over moderate high heat until it starts to shimmer Put in onion and 1/2 teaspoon salt and cook until tender, approximately five minutes.
3. Mix in garlic, chipotle, and oregano and cook until aromatic, approximately half a minute. Mix in tomato sauce, water, and toasted chiles, bring to simmer, and cook until chiles become tender, approximately ten minutes.
4. Move mixture to blender and pulse until smooth, approximately half a minute. Return sauce to now empty pot and mix in shrimp.
5. Cover and cook over moderate low heat until shrimp are thoroughly cooked and completely opaque, five to seven minutes.

6. Move shrimp to separate plates. Stir cilantro and lime juice into sauce and sprinkle with salt and pepper to taste.
7. Ladle sauce over shrimp, sprinkle with extra oil, and serve with lime wedges.

Grilled Shrimp Skewers

Ingredients

For the marinade:

- 1/2 teaspoon ground ginger
- 1/2 teaspoon salt
- 1/2 teaspoon smoked paprika
- 1 teaspoon grated lime zest
- 1/4 teaspoon cayenne pepper
- 1/2 teaspoon ground cumin
- 3 tablespoons extra-virgin olive oil
- 6 garlic cloves, minced

For the shrimps:

- 2 pounds extra-large shrim peeled and deveined
- 1/2 Teaspoon Sugar
- 1 Tablespoon Minced Fresh Cilantro
- Lime Wedges

Procedure

For the marinade:

Beat all ingredients together in medium bowl.

For the shrimps:

1. Pat shrimp dry using paper towels. Using sharp paring knife, make shallow cut down outside curve of shrimp. Put in shrimp to a container with marinade and toss to coat. Cover and put in the fridge for minimum half an hour or maximum 1 hour.

2. With a charcoal grill, open bottom vent fully. Light large chimney starter filled with charcoal briquettes (6 quarts). When top coals are partly covered with ash, pour uniformly over half of grill.

3. Set cooking grate in place, cover, and open lid vent fully. Heat grill until hot, approximately five minutes.

4. Clean and oil cooking grate. Thread shrimp tightly onto four 12-inch metal skewers (about 12 shrimp per skewer), alternating direction of heads and tails.

5. Sprinkle 1 side of skewered shrimp with sugar. Place shrimp skewers sugared side down on grill (on hotter side if using charcoal). Cook (covered if using gas), without moving them, until mildly charred on first side, three to five minutes.

6. Flip skewers and move to cooler side of grill (if using charcoal) or turn all burners off (if using gas) and cook, covered, until shrimp are opaque throughout, 1 to 2 minutes.

7. Using tongs, slide shrimp off skewers onto serving platter and sprinkle with salt and pepper to taste.

8. Sprinkle with cilantro and serve with lime wedges.

Shrimp Balls

Ingredients

- 2 pounds small shrimps, shelled, cleaned, and roughly chopped

For the tomato broth:

- 1 cup peeled, diced potatoes (about 6 ounces)
- 2 cups water
- 1 tbsp peppercorns
- 2 cups peeled and diced chayote (eight ounces)
- 1/8 teaspoon coriander seeds
- 1/3 cup finely chopped white onion
- 1 cup nopales, cooked
- 2 pounds tomatoes, finely chopped (four cups)
- 2 teaspoons salt, or to taste
- 2 garlic cloves, finely chopped
- 2 tablespoons vegetable oil

Shrimp ball seasoning

- 1/4 teaspoon coriander seeds
- 2 garlic cloves
- 1/4 teaspoon peppercorns
- 1/2 ancho chile, veins and seeds removed
- 1/2-inch piece of cinnamon stick, broken up
- 2 teaspoons salt, or to taste
- 3 tablespoons water
- 1 tablespoon vegetable oil

Procedure

1. Place the shrimps into the freezer for approximately 2 hours, until they are slightly
2. frozen (this will make it easier to grind them in the blender or food processor).
3. In the meantime, prepare the tomato broth. In a wide, heavy pan, heat the oil and fry the tomatoes, onion, and garlic.

4. Stir them occasionally and scraping the bottom of the pan, until they are reduced to a thick sauce. Put in the 4 cups of water, salt, peppercorns, and coriander seeds and bring to its boiling point.

5. Put in the potatoes and cook for approximately ten minutes, then put in the chayote and cook until nearly soft, approximately fifteen minutes more. Put in the nopales and just heat through. Tweak the seasoning.

6. Prepare the seasoning for the shrimp balls by first soaking the ancho chile in hot water for fifteen minutes, then drain and put in a blender jar. Crush the coriander seeds, peppercorns, and cinnamon stick.

7. Put in the spices to the blender jar, together with the salt, garlic, and water, and blend to a paste. Heat the oil and fry the seasoning paste using high heat for approximately 2 minutes. Set aside.

8. Combine the slightly frozen shrimps to a quite smooth consistency. Put in the fried seasoning and work it in well with your hands.

9. Lightly grease your hands, then make the mixture into balls approximately 11/4 inches (3.5 cm) in diameter—there must be 18 of them.

10. Cautiously place the shrimp balls into the simmering broth, then cover the pan and continue simmering for approximately fifteen minutes, turning them once during the cooking time.

11. Serve the shrimp balls in deep soup bowls, with sufficient the broth and vegetables.

Sauced Shrimp Crepes

Serves 6 pax

Ingredients

- 1/3 cup vegetable oil
- 1/2 teaspoon granulated sugar
- 2 cups grated chihuahua cheese or muenster
- 2 tablespoons crudely chopped white onion
- 2 pasilla chiles, wiped clean, seeds and veins removed
- Salt to taste
- 2 cups thick sour cream, plus extra for serving
- 2 pounds small shrimps cooked and peeled
- 2 pounds tomatoes, broiled
- 12 thin crepes, approximately 5 inches in diameter, prepared in accordance with any standard crepe recipe

Procedure

1. Preheat your oven to 350° f (180° c).
2. Heat a griddle or comal and toast the chiles lightly, turning them occasionally so that they do not burn. Crush the chiles into a blender jar, put in the tomatoes and onion, and blend to a smooth sauce.
3. Heat the oil in a big frying pan. Put in the sauce, sugar, and salt, and cook the mixture on moderate heat, stirring it occasionally to prevent sticking.
4. You will probably have to cover the pan with a lid, as the sauce splatters rather fiercely. After about ten minutes the sauce will have thickened and seasoned. Set it aside to cool a little.
5. Mix the sour cream well into the sauce and allow it to continue to heat through for one minute or so.
6. Combine the shrimps into 1 cup of the sauce. Put a little of the mixture in each of the crepes and roll them up loosely.
7. Put the crepes side by side on an ovenproof serving dish and pour the rest of the sauce over them.

8. Drizzle the grated cheese over the sauce and put some dollops of sour cream around the edge of the dish. Allow the crepes heat through in your oven and the cheese melt.

9. Serve instantly.

Shrimp Fajitas

Ingredients

- 1 big red onion, halved and cut thin
- 1 teaspoon cumin seeds
- 1 teaspoon minced chipotle chile in adobo sauce
- 1 teaspoon sugar
- 1/8 teaspoon cayenne pepper
- 1/4 cup minced fresh cilantro
- 2 garlic cloves, peeled and smashed
- 2 tablespoons vegetable oil
- 1/2 cup Mexican crema
- 2 pounds medium big shrimp (31 to 40 per pound), peeled, deveined, and tails removed
- 12 (6 inches) flour tortillas, warmed
- 3 red bell peppers, stemmed, seeded, and cut thin
- 4 tablespoons lime juice, plus wedges for serving
- 2 tablespoons water
- Salt and pepper

Procedure

1. Whisk 3 tablespoons oil, lime juice, garlic, chipotle, sugar, 1/2 teaspoon cumin seeds, 1 teaspoon salt, 1/2 teaspoon pepper, and cayenne together in big container. Put in shrimp and toss to coat. Cover and place in your fridge for half an hour

2. Heat 1 tablespoon oil in 12 inches nonstick frying pan over moderate high heat until it starts to shimmer

3. Put in bell peppers, onion, water, remaining 1/2 teaspoon cumin seeds, and 1/2 teaspoon salt and cook until peppers are tender and onion is browned, approximately eight minutes.

4. Move to serving container and sprinkle with salt and pepper to taste.

5. Wipe out frying pan using paper towels. Remove garlic from shrimp marinade and discard.

6. Heat 1 tablespoon oil in now empty frying pan using high heat until just smoking. Put in half of shrimp to pan in single layer and cook until spotty brown and edges turn pink, one to two minutes.

7. Remove pan from heat and flip each shrimp over using tongs. Cover and let shrimp stand off heat until just thoroughly cooked, one to two minutes; move to container and cover to keep warm.
8. Repeat with remaining 1 tablespoon oil and remaining shrimp.
9. Toss shrimp with cilantro and serve with vegetables, warm tortillas, crema, and lime wedges.

Shrimps in Ceviche

Ingredients

- 1 garlic clove, minced
- 1 jalapeño chile, stemmed, seeded, and minced
- 1/4 cup extra virgin olive oil
- 1/2 cup lemon juice (3 lemons)
- 1/2 teaspoon sugar
- 1 pound extra big shrimp (21 to 25 per pound), peeled, deveined, tails removed, and halved along the length
- 3 tablespoons minced fresh cilantro
- 2 scallions, cut thin
- Salt and pepper
- 1 teaspoon grated lime zest plus 1/2 cup juice (4 limes)
- 1 tomato, cored, seeded, and chopped fine

Procedure

1. Mix tomato, lemon juice, jalapeño, lime zest and juice, garlic, and 1/2 teaspoon salt in medium container.
2. Mix in shrimp, cover, and place in your fridge until shrimp are firm and opaque throughout, forty-five minutes to an hour, stirring midway through refrigerating.
3. Drain shrimp mixture in colander, leaving shrimp slightly wet, and move to serving container. Mix in oil, scallions, cilantro, and sugar.
4. Sprinkle with salt and pepper to taste and serve.

Marinara Sauce

Serves 2 cups

Ingredients

- 3 tablespoons extra-virgin olive oil
- Sugar, salt and pepper
- 1/3 cup dry red wine
- 1 onion, chopped fine
- 2 (28-ounce) cans whole peeled tomatoes
- 2 garlic cloves, minced
- 2 teaspoons minced fresh oregano or 1/2 teaspoon dried
- 2 tablespoons chopped fresh basil

Procedure

1. Drain tomatoes using a fine-mesh strainer set over big container.
2. Using hands, open tomatoes and remove and discard seeds and fibrous cores; let tomatoes drain, approximately five minutes.
3. Reserve 3/4 cup tomatoes separately. Reserve 21/2 cups drained tomato juice; discard extra juice.
4. Heat 2 tablespoons oil in 12-inch frying pan on moderate heat until it starts to
5. shimmer. Put in onion and cook till they become tender and lightly browned, 5 to 7 minutes. Mix in garlic and oregano and cook until aromatic, approximately half a minute.
6. Mix in remaining drained tomatoes and increase heat to medium-high. Cook, stirring frequently, until liquid has evaporated and tomatoes begin to brown and stick to pan, 10 to 12 minutes.
7. Mix in wine and cook until thick and syrupy, about 1 minute. Mix in reserved tomato juice, scraping up any browned bits.
8. Bring to simmer and cook, stirring intermittently, until sauce is thickened, eight to ten minutes.
9. Move sauce to your food processor, put in reserved 3/4 cup tomatoes, and pulse until slightly chunky, approximately 8 pulses.
10. Return sauce to now-empty skillet, mix in basil and remaining 1 tablespoon oil, and season with salt, pepper, and sugar to taste.
11. While you toss sauce with cooked pasta, gradually pour in some pasta cooking water as required to regulate consistency.

Raw Tomatoes Sauce

Serves 2 cups

Ingredients

- 1/4 cup extra-virgin olive oil
- 1 garlic clove, minced
- 1 shallot, minced
- 5 pounds very ripe tomatoes, cored and cut into 1/2-inch pieces
- 2 teaspoons lemon juice, plus extra as required
- 2 tablespoons chopped fresh basil
- Sugar, salt and pepper

Procedure

1. Stir oil, lemon juice, shallot, garlic, 1 teaspoon salt, 1/4 teaspoon pepper, and pinch sugar together in a big container.
2. Mix in tomatoes and allow to marinate until very soft and flavorful, approximately half an hour.
3. Before you serve, mix in basil and season with salt, pepper, sugar, and extra lemon juice to taste.
4. While you toss sauce with cooked pasta, gradually pour in some pasta cooking water as required to regulate consistency.
5. This sauce is perfect to garnish any kind of shrimp.

Tahini Yogurt

Ingredients

- 1/3 cup tahini
- 1 garlic clove, minced
- 1/4 cup water
- 1/3 cup plain Greek yogurt 3 tablespoons lemon juice Salt and pepper

Procedure

1. Beat tahini, yogurt, water, lemon juice, garlic, and 3/4 teaspoon salt together in a container until combined.
2. Sprinkle with salt and pepper to taste. Allow to sit until flavors blend, approximately half an hour.
3. This sauce is perfect to garnish any kind of shrimp.

Cucumber Yogurt

Serves 2 cups

Ingredients

- 1 cucumber, peeled, halved along the length, seeded, and shredded
- 1 garlic clove, minced
- 3 tablespoons extra-virgin olive oil
- 2 tablespoons minced fresh dill
- 1 cup plain Greek yogurt Cilantro, mint, parsley, or tarragon can be substituted for the dill if desired.
- Salt and pepper

Procedure

1. Beat yogurt, oil, dill, and garlic together in a moderate-sized container until combined.
2. Mix in cucumber and sprinkle with salt and pepper to taste.
3. This sauce is perfect to garnish any kind of shrimp.

Garlic Aïoli

Ingredients

- 2 teaspoons lemon juice
- 1/4 cup extra-virgin olive oil
- 3/4 cup vegetable oil
- 1 garlic clove, minced
- 1 tablespoon water
- 2 large egg yolks
- 2 teaspoons Dijon mustard
- A combination of vegetable oil and extra-virgin olive oil is crucial to the flavor of the aïoli.
- Salt and pepper

Procedure

1. Process egg yolks, mustard, lemon juice, and garlic using a food processor until combined, about 10 seconds.
2. While your food processor runs slowly drizzle in vegetable oil, approximately one minute.
3. Move mixture to medium bowl and beat in water, 1/2 teaspoon salt, and 1/4 teaspoon pepper.
4. Whisking continuously, slowly drizzle in olive oil until completely blended.
5. This sauce is perfect to garnish any kind of shrimp.
6. This sauce is perfect to garnish any kind of shrimp.

Sweet and Sour Cranberry Bean Sauce

Serves 7 pax

Ingredients

- 1/2 fennel bulb, 2 tablespoons fronds chopped, stalks discarded, bulb cored and chopped
- 1 cup plus 2 tablespoons red wine vinegar
- 1 pound (2 cups) dried cranberry beans, picked over and rinsed
- 1/2 cup pine nuts, toasted
- 1/2 cup sugar
- 1 teaspoon fennel seeds
- 3 tablespoons extra-virgin olive oil
- 6 ounces seedless red grapes, halved (1 cup)
- Salt and pepper

Procedure

1. Dissolve 3 tablespoons salt in 4 quarts cold water in large container. Put in beans and soak at room temperature for minimum 8 hours or for maximum 24 hours. Drain and wash thoroughly.
2. Bring beans, 4 quarts water, and 1 teaspoon salt to boil in a Dutch oven. Decrease the heat to a simmer and cook, stirring intermittently, until beans are tender, 1 to 2 hours. Drain beans and set aside.
3. Wipe Dutch oven clean using paper towels. Heat oil in now-empty pot on moderate heat until it starts to shimmer.
4. Put in fennel, 1/4 teaspoon salt, and 1/4 teaspoon pepper and cook till they become tender, approximately five minutes. Mix in 1 cup vinegar, sugar, and fennel seeds until sugar is dissolved.
5. Bring to simmer and cook until liquid becomes thick to syrupy glaze and edges of fennel are starting to brown, about 10 minutes.
6. Put in beans to vinegar-fennel mixture and toss to coat. Move to big container and allow to cool to room temperature.
7. Put in grapes, pine nuts, fennel fronds, and remaining 2 tablespoons vinegar and toss to combine.
8. Sprinkle with salt and pepper to taste and serve.
9. This sauce is perfect to garnish any kind of shrimp.

Shrimps Broad Bean Salad

Ingredients

- 1 large tomato, deseeded and chopped
- 2 cups peeled and steamed shrimps
- 1 large handful of fresh basil, stems removed, chopped
- A few sprigs of flat-leaf parsley, stems removed, chopped
- 2 mugs of broad beans (as broad beans like plenty of pod space, this means you'll need about 4 large handfuls of pods)
- 2 stalks of celery, diced
- 2 garlic cloves, peeled and finely minced
- Juice of $1/2$ lemon
- 1 glug of olive oil
- Salt and freshly ground black pepper

Procedure

1. Remove the beans from their cosy pods and simmer them in salted water for about 5 minutes.
2. Drain and then run cold water over them for 30 seconds or so.
3. Combine the salad ingredients together in a bowl and add the beans.
4. Mix the dressing ingredients and the shrimps together well and mix with the bean salad.
5. Season with salt and pepper to taste.

Shrimps with Pumpkin Seeds Sauce

Ingredients

- 1 small bunch cilantro, roughly chopped
- 1 tablespoon unsalted butter
- 1 teaspoon salt, or to taste
- 2 pounds medium-size shrimps, unshelled
- 1/2 small white onion, roughly chopped
- 2/3 cup thick sour cream
- 1 cup hulled, raw pumpkin seeds 2 cups cold water
- 2 fresh serrano chiles, roughly chopped with seeds

Procedure

1. Shell and devein the shrimps and save for later. Place the shells, tails, and heads, if any, into a deep cooking pan, put in the water with salt, and cook on moderate heat for approximately twenty minutes, to extract the flavor and make a light broth.

2. Strain and discard the shells, saving for later the cooking liquid. Allow the liquid to cool a little. Put in the shrimps and cook over gentle heat for approximately 3 minutes, or until they are just turning opaque. Drain the shrimps, saving for later the broth.

3. In a heavy, ungreased frying pan, toast the pumpkin seeds lightly, stirring them frequently, until they start to swell up and start to pop about—do not allow them to brown.

4. Set them aside to cool and then grind them finely in a coffee/spice grinder. (they can just be added to the blender with the broth in the next step, but the sauce will not be as smooth.)

5. Put the shrimp broth, pumpkin seeds, cilantro, chiles, and onion in a blender and blend together until the desired smoothness is achieved.

6. Melt the butter in a heavy deep cooking pan. Put in the mixed pumpkin seed sauce and cook over very low heat while stirring and scraping the bottom of the pan continuously, for approximately 3 minutes.

7. Mix in the sour cream, tweak the seasoning, and just heat through—about three minutes. Then put in the shrimps and heat through for another five minutes. The sauce must be of a medium consistency. Serve instantly.

8. Serve with fresh, hot tortillas or crusty french bread. Despite the temptation to do so, it is better not to serve it on top of rice or all that lovely sauce will be sopped up and lost.

Thank you, dear fish lover.

I am glad you accepted my teachings.
These meals have been personally codified in my
worldwide trips.
I wanted to share them with you, to let people know more
about meat and how to treat it properly.

Now you had come to know about Salmon and Shrimps
in all of their shapes, let me give you one more tip.
This manual takes part of an unmissable cookbooks
collection.
These fish-based recipes, mixed to all the tastes I met
around the world, will give you a complete idea of the
possibilities this world offers to us.
You have now the opportunity to add hundreds new
elements to your cooking skills knowledge.
Check out the other books!

Ernest Pescara

CPSIA information can be obtained
at www.ICGtesting.com
Printed in the USA
BVHW041720090621
609091BV00016B/2507